KARATE WISDOM

KARATE WISDOM

Jose M. Fraguas

P.O. Box 491788, Los Angeles, CA 90049

Disclaimer
Please note that the author and publisher of this book are NOT RESPONSIBLE in any manner whatsoever for any injury that may result from practicing the techniques and/or following the instructions given within. Since the physical activities described herein may be too strenuous in nature for some readers to engage in safely, it is essential that a physician be consulted prior to training.

First published in 2006 by Empire Books.
Copyright © 2006 by Empire Books.

All rights reserved. No part of this publication may be reproduced or utilized in any form or by any means, electronic or mechanical, including photocopying, recording, or by any information storage and retrieval system, without prior written permission from Empire Books.

Empire Books
P.O. Box 491788
Los Angeles, CA 90049

First edition
06 05 04 03 02 01 00 99 98 97   1 3 5 7 9 10 8 6 4 2

Cover photo: Courtesy of Tom Muzila.

Printed in the United States of America.

Library of Congress: 2006009381
ISBN-10: 1-933901-09-8
ISBN-13: 978-1-933901-09-1

   Library of Congress Cataloging-in-Publication Data

Fraguas, Jose M.
   Karate wisdom / Jose M. Fraguas. -- 1st ed.
      p. cm.
   Includes index.
   ISBN 1-933901-09-8 (pbk. : alk. paper)
  1. Karate--Quotations, maxims, etc. 2. Karate--Philosophy. I. Title.

GV1114.3.F7153 2006
796.815'3--dc22

2006009381

"One's blow always creates a kind of hollow. A blow is successful if, at the instant of impact, the opponent's body fits into that hollow space and assumes a form precisely identical with it."

—Mishima Yukio
Japanese writer

DEDICATION

I dedicate this book to the happy memories of Taiji Kase, Teruo Hayashi and Keinosuke Enoeda who, in their very different ways, taught me to love the art of karate-do. Their laughter will be forever missed.

Acknowledgments

Many people were responsible for making this book possible, some more directly than others. I want to extend my gratitude to all those who so generously contributed their time and experience to the preparation of this work. A special thanks to designer Patrick Gross. I also want to thank France's Thierry Plee, long-time friend and president of *Sedirep* and *Budo Editions*; David Chambers, founder and editor of *Dragon Times*; Norma Harvey of England; Bill Bly, editor of *American Samurai* magazine; John Cheetham, editor of *Shotokan Karate* magazine; Arthur Tansley of Tokyo, Japan; Don Warrener, director of Rising Sun Productions; Harold E. Sharp, a true legend in the world of martial arts; Ken Yasuda, for his calligraphy skills; Alexander Chichvarin, of Russia, for his sincere support; Isaac Florentine, film director and passionate karate-ka; Silvio Dokov, excellent photographer and friend; Lance Webster, editor of the work; and finally to my wife, Julie, whose discernment is always tempered with kindness.

A word of appreciation is also due to my good friend Masahiro Ide, president of *JK Fan* and *Champ* videos, for his generosity and cooperation in this project; I also want to thank Okuma-san from the JKA Honbu Dojo in Tokyo for his assistance, kindness and supply of great photographic material for some of the chapters; and I must acknowledge the publishers of *Gekkan Karate-do* magazine [Fukushodo, Ltd., Japan].

And last but not least, to all my instructors, past and present, for giving me the understanding and knowledge to undertake all the martial arts projects I've done during my life. My understanding of the art has grown over the years, thanks, in great part, to the questions they made me ask myself.

You all have my enduring thanks.

—Jose M. Fraguas

About the Author

Born and raised in Madrid, Spain, Jose M. Fraguas began his martial arts studies with judo, in grade school, at the age of 9. From there, he moved to tae-kwondo and then to kenpo-karate, earning a black belt in both styles. During this same period, he also studied shito-ryu karate under Japanese masters Yasunari Ishimi and Masahiro Okada. Fraguas eventually received a fifth-degree black belt and the title of *Shihan* from Soke Mabuni Kenzo. He began his career as a writer at age 16 by serving as a regular contributor to martial arts magazines in Great Britain, France, Spain, Italy, Germany, Portugal, Holland and Australia. Having a black belt in three different styles allows him to better reflect the physical side of the martial arts in his writing: "Feeling before writing," Fraguas says.

In 1986, Fraguas founded his own book and magazine company in Europe, authoring dozens of books and distributing his magazines to 35 countries in three different languages. His reputation and credibility as a martial artist and publisher became well known to the top masters around the world. Considering himself a martial artist first and a writer and publisher second, Fraguas feels fortunate to have had the opportunity to interview many legendary martial arts teachers. He recognizes that much of the information given in the interviews helped him to discover new dimensions in the martial arts. "I was constantly absorbing knowledge from the great masters," he recalls. "I only trained with a few of them, but intellectually and spiritually all of them have made very important contributions to my growth as a complete martial artist."

Steeped in tradition yet looking to the future, Fraguas understands and appreciates martial arts history and philosophy and feels this rich heritage is a necessary steppingstone to personal growth and spiritual evolution. His desire to promote both ancient philosophy and modern thinking provided the motivation for writing this book. "If the motivation is just money, a book cannot be of good quality," Fraguas says. "If the book is written to just make people happy, it cannot be deep. I want to write books so I can learn as well as teach. Karate-do, like human life itself, is filled with experiences that seem quite ordinary at the time and assume a fable stature only with the passage of the years. I hope this work will be appreciated by future practitioners of the art of the empty-hand."

The author is currently living in Los Angeles, California. He can be contacted at: **mastersseries@yahoo.com.**

Introduction

As early as I can remember, my house was filled with books. Many of these books—some new, some old—were excellent collections of quotations. My father and mother clipped quotes from magazines or newspapers, and even wrote some themselves and posted them on kitchen cabinets, the refrigerator and other special places for the family to see.

There are many pleasures to be derived from a book on quotations. There is the relief of finding something that has been buzzing in our minds, there is also the pleasure of finding some thought of which we approve but which we have not managed to express clearly and there is a purely retrospective delight. Of course, wisdom is meaningless until our own experience has given it meaning.

Through my childhood, reading and rereading these quotes has helped me to replace negatives thoughts with strong and positive alternatives. While words are not substitutes for the difficult physical and mental training required to master the art of karate-do, they are a relevant aspect of the transmission and the learning process of every student. *Karate Wisdom* is an anthology of the best words said by the great masters of the art of the "empty hand." It is organized into several interconnected chapters, examining different elements of the art, including its tradition, philosophy, general training, sport competition, kata, kumite, makiwara practice and weaponry training.

All the masters have expressed similar ideas in very different ways. Regardless of the words they used, there must be truth in the philosophies and principles that so many different people have believed in and lived by—and in some cases—died for. The more I researched, the more I realized that those great masters are more like you and me than they are different. They had difficult days and seemingly impossible hurdles, yet they endured and prevailed.

I have made every effort to present each quotation within its con-

text as accurately as possible. In philosophical matters, it is syntax—more than vocabulary—that needs to be corrected. Due to the limitations of language and linguistic expression when dealing with philosophical and spiritual matters, it is easy to understand why some of the ideas and principles of these masters are so complex, subtle and intricate—particularly if the ideas are studied out of context. If you try to apply some of these ideas to your own life, don't forget that it is easier to quote somebody else than it is to really understand what they meant by saying it. There are obvious dangers in using words without being sure what we really mean. But there is another less obvious danger in trying to provide exact definitions—the danger is that we may think we have succeeded. As the philosopher Bertrand Russell wrote: "There is no more reason why a person who uses a word correctly should be able to tell what it means than there is why a planet which is moving correctly should know Kepler's laws." I respectfully would like to advise the reader to *listen* not to the words of the masters but to *what* they really meant when they said those words. The way of karate-do produces a practitioner torn between the art and the mystic. The way of the artist and the way of the mystic are similar, but the mystic lacks a craft ... the physical techniques. The craft (physical training) keeps the artist in touch with the remarkableness of the world and in relationship to it. Therefore, philosophy without hard physical training is useless.

This book originated more than 20 years ago as a personal manuscript of life-affirming quotations taken from legendary karate masters for my own personal use. As I had the great opportunity to keep interviewing many of the greatest karate-ka in the world, the pages of the manuscript kept increasing until one day my mother asked me: "What are you planning to do with all these quotations?" As soon as I answered, "I don't know," she was pointing with her finger to the shelves of one of the bookcases at home where the complete collection of books on quotations was. She simply smiled and left the room.

Meeting the masters and having long conversations with them allowed me to do more than simply scratch the surface of the technical aspects of their respective styles. It also helped me to research and analyze the human beings behind the teachers.

Years before anyone ever heard of any of them, they devoted themselves to their arts, often in solitude, sometimes to the exclusion of other pursuits most of us take for granted. They worked themselves into extraordinary physical condition and stayed there. They ignored distractions and diversions and brought to their training a great deal of concentration. The best of them got as good as they could possibly get at performing and teaching their chosen art, and the rest of us watched them and, leading our balanced lives, wondered how good we might have gotten at something had we devoted ourselves to whatever we did as ferociously as these masters embraced their arts. In that respect, they bear our dreams.

Most of what passed as human wisdom is merely the post-examination gabble of excited individuals trying to guess how the new lessons will explain the old questions of life and Budo training. Anything is fresh on the first hearing ... even though others may have heard it a thousand times through a score of generations.

In the spring of 2002, I finished the first draft of this work, took the manuscript and sent it to several karate masters. It was exciting to hear their comments. Many of them wrote kind words that they wanted me to use to support the project. Unfortunately, some of them won't see the final printed work, because they shed their mortal skin and returned to the sacred battlefields where the true warriors fight their battles. Their words are in this book because without them this work would never be completed.

More than three decades after my mother pointed to that old bookcase, here is the final work. Books are an essential part of my life and they have opened new and exciting avenues of life. My goal is to share these thoughts with as many people as possible. I hope this collection provides comfort and inspiration for the karate practitioner, the martial artist—regardless of style—and for the casual browser and reader. If you, the reader, find this work useful as both a guide and a reference work and discover some unexpected sayings, the book will have served its purpose.

Enjoy.

—Jose M. Fraguas

CONTENTS

15 TRADITION
伝統

69 TRAINING
修業

131 KATA
形

169 KUMITE
組手

185 SPORT
試合

217 MAKIWARA
まきわら

229 PHILOSOPHY
哲学

311 KOBUDO
小武道

Tradition

伝統

Karate Wisdom

Hayashi Sensei was a true kata encyclopedia. His historical and technical knowledge was second to none—a true master of his own right.
Alex Sternberg

The beauty of karate is that it has unlimited space for developing. Of course, I don't learn new techniques, but there are endless subtleties and levels of understanding in the existing ones.
Avi Rokah

The teachers were very few and everything was very limiting. The spirit was very different than today. It was more of a martial art and less a sport. The training sessions were tough and "martial" compared to what we have today's karate.
Dominique Valera

It's hard for me to accept that after having the privilege of training and learning from these men that I need to shop around a little more. When I was a young person and began training at the Nagamine Dojo, I often wondered what it was like for him training when he was my age.
Eihachi Ota

Master Funakoshi was very old when I met him, but one thing that I still recall is that once he put the gi on, his whole attitude and body movement changed immediately. It was like he received some kind of

external energy by wearing the karate gi. The transformation in his physical movements was amazing.
Keinosuke Enoeda

Karate is one entity. It should not be separated into categories. I have never learned or taught a class in that manner. I try to teach a more complete karate.
Hideharu Igaki

However, the nature of the fighting in Japan was radically different from that in the West. The competition was more blood and guts. There was no safety equipment. Broken bones, knockouts, and an assortment of other injuries were commonplace. The Japanese style of fighting was based on stability. They charged straight ahead, never backed up, and never quit. Back-fists were rarely scored as points, and the hit-and-run tactics of the mobile fighters were never seen.
Katsutaka Tanaka

Doshisha University Karate Club sought instruction from Master Kenwa Mabuni, who had settled in nearby Osaka, following the advice of Master Miyagi who could not stay in mainland Japan all the time.
Keiji Tomiyama

This integration of Funakoshi, Motobu, and Mabuni teachings

Karate Wisdom

provide the ryobu-kai practitioner with a very flexible and adaptable method.
Kiyoshi Yamazaki

Karate was all I could think of and it was then when I decided to study goju-ryu and shotokan. Although I was doing very good I was not completely happy with what I had and decided to develop my own way of doing karate. I then created my own style that I called "kyokushinkai."
Mas Oyama

My family has always been involved in Budo. My great grandfather was a great yokozuna, the most prestigious title in sumo circles. My uncle, Mr. Togashi, was a 9th degree black belt in judo and my other uncle, Mr. Yano, a master in the Japanese fencing art of kendo. My father was a 5th black belt degree in judo and an expert in the weaponry art of naginata.
Yoshinao Nanbu

Duplicating what you have been taught without thinking and analyzing what you're doing, is just to follow blindly—that not the right attitude of Budo. You are supposed to use the art to elevate and grow, but not to follow without thinking for yourself. In the true expression of any art form a copy has no worth, only originals have value.
Yuishi Negishi

Every karate-do style is simply the personal perception of an individuals idea of how to do things. You must be careful and not jump from one style to another other but it is definitely good to be able to use different approaches to combat.
Seiji Mishimura

TRADITION

The style of karate I learned and taught is shorinji-ryu, Yabu Kentsul's style. This is why my katas are named like Yabu Chinto's. Of course, over the years I have refined the kata, as karate in those early years was quite unsophisticated. There weren't even any real names of styles in the early days—it was just called "te."
Richard Kim

Training was often a macho thing in some dojos then, and people routinely got teeth knocked out, broken bones, and worse. I don't call that "traditional," though. I call it stupid.
Randall Hassell

All I learned during the first year under Master Kyan was how to clean the floors and carry water from one place to another. There was no karate training at all—no punching or kicking—just cleaning. This was the way the old teachers used to find out how dedicated and loyal you were.
Shinpo Matayoshi

My impression that first training session was an example of a true warrior's spirit and the practice resembled that of a real fight. The tidal wave of energy I felt from that practice made the hair on the back of my neck stand up. They were fighting standing, against the wall and on the ground grappling. I knew right there that this was the type of spirit and training I wanted.
Tom Muzila

Often the dojo was in half darkness. The purpose was to give us an instinct and feel against unknown attackers. We were totally devoted to the art—the attitude and approach to training was very different than what you see today.
Tamas Weber

Karate Wisdom

Soke Kubota recognized my passion for karate and offered to let me clean the dojo twice a week in exchange for training.
Val Mijailovic

Overall, in the early years, Westerners welcomed traditional training with a positive attitude. It was something new and different. I believe that the people who were not afraid to work hard gained by training in the Japanese tradition.
Wally Slocki

The art of karate is gaining international recognition now—but this has nothing to do with how I was taught in the past by my teachers.
Gogen Yamaguchi

Coming from a goju-ryu background we used to do a lot of physical conditioning exercises for the body. The idea was to make the body strong to take a blow and to deliver a powerful strike of your own. It was very hard on the body.
Yoshiaki Ajari

Many of the American instructors I know have a broader overview of karate than their Japanese counterpart. The Japanese, however, in many cases are better trained in the basics than many Americans. Many of the Japanese will work a few basics for months or years. Most Americans always want to learn something new.
Bill Dometrich

Tradition

For many years I was pretty much on my own. By this I mean I didn't belong to any organization. I did not change anything but I had to adjust certain things to being by myself. I was teaching my students exactly what I was taught by my teachers. I never created, invented or developed a new style.
Chuck Merriman

One of my greatest sensei and an inspiration to me was shito-ryu master Ryusho Sakagami. This man was a dictionary of kata and a great, but humble person.
Dan Ivan

I consider myself a Master Ryusho Sakagami student. I don't look at myself as a master at all. Today everybody wants recognition; everybody wants to be called "master."
Fumio Demura

There are many Westerners who enjoy the paramilitary approach because it provides a form of emotional security. I think it is all a bit adolescent actually, and when you grow up you really shouldn't need that kind of thing as much.
Harry Cook

I started with Master Kosei Kuniba and then I studied the goju-ryu style under Master Seko Higa. He taught a great deal and I progressed very consistently for a long time. But then I decided to go to Okinawa to train.
Teruo Hayashi

Karate Wisdom

The Japanese masters considered, to my embarrassment, that I had mastered the true spirit of karate to a level where no one could honestly judge me, based on my intuitive and mental focus, because there were no longer any limits to what I felt I could achieve. I believe that this demonstrates the importance of practicing honestly and deeply without dreaming of quick successes or fast belt grades.
Henri Plee

I started under An'ichi Miyagi who was running Grandmaster Chojun Miyagi's school—the original garden dojo. I felt in love with goju-ryu on the very first day. I started to train up to six hours a day!
Morio Higaonna

I used to collect Sensei Funakoshi to go to training. Both the atmosphere and the spirit at the old dojo was very special—very different from the other schools. I firmly believe that there was some kind of magic there.
Taiji Kase

My father's teaching was based on the principles of "shin," "gi" and "tai." "Shin" means heart, "gi" means technique, and "tai" means body. The practitioner should look for a perfect balance among these three aspects. Unfortunately, many of today's karate-ka fail to balance these elements properly.
Kenei Mabuni

The training was very hard and there was a high level of dropouts, particularly during the first year.
Takayuki Mikami

At the first class, the beginners were taken outside where the makiwara posts were standing. We had to hit them until the skin on our knuckles came off.
Minobu Miki

TRADITION

Budo was part of my family. My grandfather belonged to the Sanada clan of samurai. Budo was always present in my education. My father was a disciplinarian since he was a military man.
Masatoshi Nakayama

To me it's sad to see how many good karate-do practitioners ignore how to coach or instruct in a professional way. It is not enough for the teacher to demonstrate the technique and for the students to repeat it in the old way.
Hidetaka Nishiyama

Usually, Master Nakayama led the classes. Master Funakoshi would sit down and tell Nakayama Sensei what to do. He was always there observing.
Teruyuki Okazaki

The training became more severe than military discipline. In the military, superiors could beat subordinates with a bo, or order troop punishment but in karate we would be left sitting in seiza for hours, forbidden to move.
Osamu Ozawa

There is an ancient Chinese maxim which says, "On ko chi shin." This means, "To study the old is to understand the new." In short, the "Bubishi" is the Bible of karate tradition—irrespective of modern interpretations—as all "styles" rest upon identical principles influenced only by various interpretations of "common" knowledge.
Patrick McCarthy

In the beginning, when I saw Nishiyama Sensei perform, I was not quite sure about him as he could not speak English. It was broken English and I couldn't understand what he was saying. I just copied him.
Ray Dalke

Karate Wisdom

Nakaima Sensei's whole philosophy was to attack the opponent without allowing him to react. He stressed striking combinations and said karate-ka should never let the opponent perceive our breathing pattern—otherwise, they are dead.
Tsuguo Sakumoto

In 1965 I invited Enoeda, Shirai, Kanazawa and Kase senseis to South Africa. They went to teach in different areas and later on we had the first South African Championship. What was really interesting to me is that right after winning both the kata and kumite divisions they told me I should retire and concentrate on judging and teaching. They made me realize that I needed to support the art from a different perspective.
Stan Schmidt

My teacher told all the students that we must toughen our bodies and make them strong so we could attack anyone. I remember we had no makiwara at all, so we used rocks. I recall hitting one wrong and cutting my hand pretty badly.
Takayuki Kubota

Yamaguchi Sensei was a towering strength of the goju-ryu foundation ... without question. I've had the privilege of living under his roof, training with him personally and getting placed in a position of relative importance. I have since gone independently on to pursue further study with the Okinawan masters.
Tino Ceberano

Tradition

Be true to yourself, your family, your country and humanity. Do not separate karate from your life. Find what lights up your life and link karate to it.
Tatsuo Hirano

Zen meditation was important to the samurai about 800 years ago. They called it the martial arts of moving Zen.
Tsutomu Ohshima

At Omoto Sensei's dojo, after class my teacher would talk to me about how to be a samurai, not only how to fight, but also about the martial artist's etiquette and knowledge. This is called "bushi no tashinami."
Akio Minakami

The karate masters upheld the old karate values and standards and placed great emphasis on dojo-kun (etiquette). They took pride in patiently teaching their national art to Westerners, as well as Okinawans. Karate was presented in a dignified, strict manner. To a Westerner, it appeared fascinating, challenging and mysterious.
Anthony Mirakian

All the traditional martial arts approach both the "do" and "jutsu" of their art from a specific, philosophical and physical perspective. As we progress, we develop more depth, greater skills, greater fluidity, and greater fluency in our ability to understand and use the art. But the essential principles that are unique to that art remain the same.
Edmond Otis

Karate Wisdom

It was very stressful growing up as the son of one of the most famous Japanese karate-ka, Grandmaster Gogen Yamaguchi, because everybody said, "You are the son of Gogen Yamaguchi." So, I couldn't choose my own life.
Goshi Yamaguchi

In Budo and traditional karate, good students never break away from their teacher. There is no reason to do this like there is no reason for a son to break away from his father or mother.
H. Ohtsuka II

The karate practitioner needs to understand that he needs to drastically change his attitude when his life is at stake. He has to be able to switch on—at will—and reach a point in which he can do what has to be done to preserve his life.
Hajimu Takashima

Nowadays, it seems like everything is a race to the higher ranking and a run on the money wagon. It is sad, but there are not that many real Budo-ka who practice and teach the martial arts as a way of life.
Jon Bluming

Traditional Japanese training means students have to do kihon drills everyday, and they have to be done with manners and patience. The sensei never explains anything, nor does he smile.
Kunio Miyake

Master Nakayama was great because he built a JKA empire, which then the world's largest traditional karate organization. It was not only the largest but also the most solid karate organization in the 70s and 80s.
Koss Yokota

Tradition

Look at the old JKA black and white 8 millimeter movies and compare the kata of Nakayama Sensei, Kanazawa Sensei and other old masters with kata done by their students of today, and you will see that it looks like a different style with the same name.
Malcolm Dorfman

When we talk about karate as a way of life, we open the possibility of many interpretations. It is interesting that, regardless of how people understand it, there are some fundamental truths to it that don't change.
Masahiko Tanaka

Shotokan was the original style. The simple thing I teach is that karate is changing, and it is possible that it could disappear. I know karate as a martial art, but now it seems more like dancing. I would like to return to the original karate ... to its sources.
Mikio Yahara

I was informed that there was an excellent master in Osaka. His name was Kenwa Mabuni, and I began my training under him around 1935. Training at that time was very different than today. I also trained under Choki Motobu.
Ryusho Sakagami

Master Gichin Funakoshi wrote, "The ultimate aim of the art of karate lies not in victory or defeat, but in the perfection of character of its participants." He wrote this during the early 20th century, arguably the most aggressive and violent century in history.
Shojiro Koyama

Soke Hayashi used to give very little explanation about the technique. He just gave his commands to perform the techniques and the kiai. It was up to us to watch carefully when he was moving and notice the

Karate Wisdom

details of the techniques. Our ability to do this was directly related to our level of knowledge and maturity in the art.
Seinosuke Mitsuya

One day I saw Sakagami Sensei punching a tree. I asked him what he was doing, and he told me that he was practicing karate. Not long afterward I enlisted two of my friends, and we asked Sakagami Sensei to teach us.
Shigeru Sawabe

I respect my father very highly and this sense of commitment has been the guiding principle of my life.
Tetsuhiko Asai

I was the first member of my family who took the goju-ryu style of karate. My family accepted it well, but my brother gave me a hard time for a while because he thought I should have stuck to the family tradition of shorin-ryu.
Teruo Chinen

Ohtsuka Sensei was a real Japanese samurai. He had the right spirit and attitude. I have never met a man with such a great personality. He was one of the greatest karate men ... both physically and mentally.
Tatsuo Suzuki

Both Okinawa and Japanese master worked hard to establish and preserve a great style of karate. Although there are few technical

differences, the truth is these are irrelevant because the final goal of both goju-ryu versions are the same.
Yosuke Yamashita

A traditional master teaches his students according to the student's capabilities, dedication, understanding and trustworthiness. All these elements may affect the way the student receives the knowledge.
Yashunari Ishimi

My father found the techniques of "te" very similar to those of Takeuchi Ryu jujitsu. Though Arakaki was in no way a master of "te," my father found the system to be very intriguing. He quit his job and opened his own martial arts center in 1923.
Yasuhiro Konishi

The goal of Budo is to develop the practitioner as a warrior and as a human being.
Yoshiharu Osaka

Karate-do strives internally to train the mind to develop a clear conscience, enabling one to face the world honestly, while externally developing strength to the point where one may overcome even ferocious wild animals. Mind and technique become one in true karate.
Gichin Funakoshi

Gichin Funakoshi was an advocate of the spiritual aspects of Karate-do and placed much greater emphasis on this than on the techniques of fighting.
Shigeru Egami

Karate Wisdom

Karate was distinguished at that time by its hardness, toughness, and the idea of practical application. Every single technique we learned was meant to work in a real encounter. No sport, no games. The people practicing at that time were not interested in competition or finesse, they were interested in pure fighting.
Alex Sternberg

Once we arrived we went to Gogen Yamaguchi's dojo to train but he didn't accept us. We politely told him that it would be an honor for us to train in his dojo, but he refused to allow us participate.
Dominique Valera

All karate styles have the same basics—the blocks, punches, kicks, and stances. What is unique or different between styles is the delivery system for the particular body motions.
Eihachi Ota

To show respect to his fellow master, Kenwa Mabuni only taught naha-te at Doshisha University, thus the club remained a goju-ryu school.
Keiji Tomiyama

We would practice well into the night—and often kata special training was conducted at night to give the feel of using karate in the dark—and in different spaces. I was very fortunate indeed to study under him.
Kiyoshi Yamazaki

Everybody knows Master Funakoshi. I had the great pleasure of training at his dojo but his emphasis was more on philosophy and ethical principles than on fighting so I decided to part ways with him. I truly respect him very much. He was a great man.
Mas Oyama

Tradition

The training at that time was extremely tough. Very hard and physically demanding. Every day we had to do 1,000 front kicks with kiai, and punch the makiwara thousands of times, not even stopping when our knuckles were bleeding. There was no way out. No excuses to quit.
Yoshinao Nanbu

I began teaching for Monsieur Henry Plee at his school in Paris. It was there I saw many new things for the first time in my life that opened my point of view as individual.
Yoshinao Nanbu

Master Nakayama changed the positions and developed a different form of karate. He pushed the art of karate as a form of physical education, and I guess he decided to modify certain technical aspects to better serve his new goal.
Yuishi Negishi

Our martial arts culture, discipline, moral values and traditions make us what we are. If for the sake of our student's fees, we were to throw all this away, then our students would have the right to be disappointed.
Seiji Mishimura

Because of their culture. The master taught the student personally and this is the way the information was handed down—teacher to student— and in some ways this is the best.
Richard Kim

The instructors did not, by and large, willfully injure their students. The students did it to each other.
Randall Hassell

Karate Wisdom

The idea of a teacher accepting money for teaching karate was very unusual. He would not be considered a real karate teacher because according to the old bujutsu traditions, martial arts cannot be bought with money. Martial arts is a treasure—you can give it to anyone you want but you should not sell it.
Shinpo Matayoshi

A basic practice in those days was almost like, life and death survival. I would have to get so psyched up mentally to just survive a practice, without getting busted up and hit too much.
Tom Muzila

I don't think that a pure style has ever existed in real terms during the history of karate. Like painting or writing, nothing can be described as a "pure" art—everything is a combination of several influences.
Tamas Weber

Things were a bit different in those days. "Tougher" is a mild description. Being dragged across the floor like a mop was the way you learned. And if you showed pain or complained about your injury you were a dead duck. The first thing that they did was to attack any injury. So you learned not to show pain and to never complain.
Val Mijailovic

I really don't understand this idea of practicing a pure system, because there is no such thing. The people who say this think that doing the same

TRADITION

Funakoshi, Ueshiba or Kano did is to practice a pure system. Let me tell you something, if you look at what Jigoro Kano, Gichin Funakoshi and Morihei Ueshiba did, they also modified what they were taught to suit their own preferences. Even they didn't have a "pure" system.
Wally Slocki

At the university the training was very hard compared to regular dojos in the cities. In the university dojo there was not enough room for everybody, so the seniors students put a lot of pressure on the beginners to make them quit. The idea was give them a hard time so they would leave. That way we had more room for training.
Yoshiaki Ajari

The arts of Budo are very special, but at the same time we must try to not make them special. Just do them naturally, as part of life. It's not good to have false and unrealistic hopes when we train, because in the end we'll be very disappointed with ourselves.
Bill Dometrich

Budo is a "warrior way" and in Okinawa the word "bushi" means a "gentleman warrior." Gentleman is the important word here. It means the character of the person. You are a guide and example to follow and you do what you say. People judge you more by what you do than by what you say. In karate, with rank comes responsibility. This is what "do" means.
Chuck Merriman

Karate Wisdom

In my earliest years in Japan, before I was confident that my former enemies, the Japanese, wouldn't bust my head in training, I was definitely wide-eyed and cautious.
Dan Ivan

I remember that when I arrived in the United States, I had to fight a great battle against frustration because of my poor English. I recall crying in bed for more than two days because I couldn't communicate. It was very difficult for me to adapt to a new culture and language.
Fumio Demura

The real traditions of the Japanese martial arts are best seen in the classical sword and related systems, and certainly I think that Westerners respond very well to the "real" traditional approach.
Harry Cook

When I found Nakaima Kenko, his only student was his son and he had no intention of breaking that tradition. I sat in front of his house for many hours and begged for months until he decided to accept me as a disciple.
Teruo Hayashi

Grandmaster Miyagi used to teach the history of the art to An'ichi—the oral traditions and the philosophy—but not before Aichi had finished the chores of fixing the house, cleaning the garden, et cetera.
Morio Higaonna

We didn't think about tournaments or sport. It was touch and kill, very much like katana training. This was the true age of Budo!
Taiji Kase

TRADITION

An instructor has a big responsibility on his shoulders. It's important that the instructor study the way of karate-do together with his students.
Kenzo Mabuni

It was like a mission to us. We were ready to give everything we had in training. We worked extremely hard in a very difficult time for Japan, just after the war. We never looked for the easy life; our motivation for training was very, very different from the practitioners today.
Takayuki Mikami

Very soon I realized that it was not as simple as I thought. That day I had my first challenge of trying to perfect the karate movements—and I still have that feeling of wanting to perfect karate inside of me.
Masatoshi Nakayama

Master Funakoshi's techniques were in principle the same as Yoshitaka's, but the external form was different. I guess some of the youngest students didn't understand that, since they were only looking at the external form.
Hidetaka Nishiyama

Master Funakoshi always stressed five important points in his teachings: the mental aspects, the physical aspects, staying calm, being exact, and being natural. He liked to explain how the human body works and how important it was to use the correct techniques to attack the right body parts.
Teruyuki Okazaki

There were some differences but not between the masters such as Yamaguchi, Funakoshi, Mabuni, et cetera. All those differences lay between the young students, and not the masters.
Osamu Ozawa

Karate Wisdom

Through studying the wisdom of the ancient masters we can better understand how and why karate is the way it is today. How many times have you re-read a passage in a book only to marvel over a newly found message?
Patrick McCarthy

To me, Nishiyama Sensei knows more about karate—the physical, the mental, the spiritual—than anybody I've seen so far. And I have seen a lot, trust me.
Ray Dalke

For two years Master Kenko taught me nothing about his style of karate—he kept me sweeping the dojo, practicing the dachi, uke, and tsuki kata. To be honest, I felt like giving up, but I am quite stubborn so I stayed.
Tsuguo Sakumoto

Karate should teach respect for your partner and opponent alike because ultimately they are one and the same. Like any human activity, karate cannot be practiced in a vacuum.
Joko Ninomiya

All Japanese teachers were very tough. Interestingly enough they were very kind outside the dojo and took a lot of time educating me in the traditional aspects and principles of Budo.
Stan Schmidt

Tradition

It is impossible to regulate the whole karate world but it is not impossible is to teach respect to the students—respect and etiquette. Unfortunately, many dojos in the West lack this. This should be preserved and passed down for future generations. Without respect and etiquette, karate is just common street brawling.
Takayuki Kubota

Modern study makes possible for an individual to make inevitable progress and development in whatever he wants and needs to excel. This stands strongly with today's practitioners ... whether they are Westerners or Asians.
Tino Ceberano

Karate-do is a dedicated practice of a combat system; it is a means and method to clean and clear your mind through the forging (kime) of spirit and body through daily training.
Tatsuo Hirano

Everything I have belongs to my students. It is not mine, regardless of how expensive the things surrounding me may be. My students gave them to me.
Tsutomu Ohshima

There were no styles before Funakoshi Sensei, Mabuni Sensei, Otsuka Sensei and Miyagi Sensei. The original Ryukyu Bujutsu, which includes what we now call sumo, bo, sai, nunchaku and empty hand fighting, was all originally called simply "te" or "ti" in Okinawan pronunciation.
Akio Minakami

Karate Wisdom

Okinawans take great pride in the teaching of karate. Karate is their national art and heritage, their cultural contribution to the world. They take pride in presenting it in a civilized and dignified manner.
Anthony Mirakian

When I was a child, I couldn't say "daddy" all the time. I had to say "sensei" or "hanshi." It was always something like that. It was not like father and son; it was always teacher and student. It was difficult.
Goshi Yamaguchi

You don't have to be physical to defeat obstacles to get what you want in life. This is the true main idea of karate.
H. Ohtsuka II

The dojo kun displays very important ethical and moral principles in the art of karate. Principles that all karate-ka should follow.
Hajimu Takashima

When you are seriously looking for a real dedicated sensei—who doesn't have to be Japanese, provided he's been through the fire on a real battle ground—find one who can teach you how to become one with yourself.
Jon Bluming

Karate has been changing rapidly for the last several decades, and it is very difficult to say that this or that style is pure.
Kunio Miyake

A qualified instructor must not only have the ranking of san-dan or above, but he must also have the proper age for maturity, which is usually about 30, and enough karate experience, normally 10 years or more.
Koss Yokota

TRADITION

The JKA, until the death of Nakayama Sensei, was without doubt the greatest karate organization in the history of karate. He developed it and held it together with his quiet magnetism and great judgment.
Malcolm Dorfman

It is important to respect and give credit to the teachers, because without them, our spiritual growth probably would never come about. And without their guidance in training, we wouldn't be who we are today.
Masahiko Tanaka

In Japan, the son is always the heir to his father's throne. Mabuni Kenei, although a junior to me, had to be the leader of his father's heritage. Kenwa Mabuni Sensei, knowing that I was a senior, suggested that I carry on with the tradition of the Itosu-ha, which I honored and accepted.
Ryusho Sakagami

Master Nakayama was the essence of modern Budo. After WWII, Master Nakayama created a new Budo, which we still follow to this day. He opened traditional karate to a much broader audience and a wider market of potential students with the advent of tournament karate.
Shojiro Koyama

The Japanese culture of yesterday, as well as the one of today, is very much interconnected with the spirit and technique of Budo.
Seinosuke Mitsuya

The teachings of Kanryo Higaonna were present in the curriculum and syllabus of Sakagami Sensei. In fact, his teachings were pretty much the same as Mabuni Kenwa's. There were no substantial differences.
Shigeru Sawabe

Karate Wisdom

To truly understand what Budo means, I would tell them to put their hearts into it and never stop training. Budo is Japanese culture, and sometimes it is hard for non-Japanese to understand.
Tetsuhiko Asai

I remember Miyagi Sensei was a stern and quiet man. His movements were very soft but extremely powerful, limber and flexible. The combination of such power and flexibility was incredible. His hand strength was incredible and his movements very precise.
Teruo Chinen

Ohtsuka Sensei was a very active individual and always enjoyed what he was doing. His techniques were very fast, especially his ura-ken [backfist]. I believe that he had formulated the wado-ryu style a few years before I started training under him.
Tatsuo Suzuki

If a person gets involved in karate simply because he wants to exercise, I don't think he really knows or cares about the important things that should be known before entering a dojo. In this case, the dojo where he ends up will strictly be an accident … mostly because the school is conveniently located near his work, home or school.
Yashunari Ishimi

TRADITION

With the help of my father, Funakoshi Sensei established a To-te practice club at Keio University, the first university karate club in Japan. My father, Funakoshi Sensei and Ohtsuka Sensei were the principal instructors. My father continued to instruct a curriculum consisting of kendo, jujitsu and western boxing at the Ryobu-Kan. Karate-jutsu was born when Funakoshi Sensei added karate to this mix. As yet, no names were applied to the emerging styles.
Yasuhiro Konishi

To search for the old is to understand the new. The old, the new, this is a matter of time. In all things man must have a clear mind. The Way: Who will pass it on straight and well?
Gichin Funakoshi

The ideal of Gichin Funakoshi, who has come to be recognized as the "Father of Karate-do," was to advance from jutsu ("technique") to Do (the "way"). It became my mission to realize this ideal.
Shigeru Egami

Karate is not an art for privileged people, it is an art for everybody. So everybody needs to have the same opportunities to achieve excellence in its practice. Therefore karate is Budo that can be practiced as a sport at a younger age.
Alex Sternberg

Karate Wisdom

I have the greatest respect for Yoshinao Nanbu. He came to Europe and instead of hiding behind the Japanese aura of mastery, he stepped onto the mat and competed in national tournaments. He was the first Japanese who really impressed me with his training.
Dominique Valera

The tradition of Budo developed not for the purpose of creating the most efficient predatory animal possible, but to develop the greatest human character.
Joko Ninomiya

Karate instructors belonging to the old generations should do more in public to promote the art. We should use interviews, magazines, books, and video to continue the legacy that was passed onto us by our teachers.
Eihachi Ota

There are many kinds of karate and karate-ka in the West as well as in Japan. Some Western people are far more advanced than some Japanese.
Keiji Tomiyama

Training in shoto-kai was very different. We never heard of tournaments, it was unthinkable. One practiced karate conditioning and kata training but sparring was something very different than what we understand today.
Kiyoshi Yamazaki

The physical training of the modern-day practitioners of the art of karate is a living legacy from this illustrious past. The physical aspects of the art are both rich and spectacular. But to be effective these powerful weapons must be under control.
Mas Oyama

TRADITION

I observed how nature works and tried to adapt those principles to the art of nanbudo. The beginnings of nanbudo were very difficult because most all my sankukai students and affiliates around the world didn't follow me into the new expression of the art.
Yoshinao Nanbu

Zen training is paramount for karate-do development. The spiritual aspect is very important when you are practicing Japanese karate. You need both to have the complete art.
Yuishi Negishi

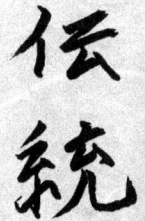

Unfortunately, many modern karate practitioners don't trust or respect each other—not only in Japan or Okinawa but all over the world. They are so proud of their own styles that they lose perspective on things. They reject anyone that doesn't use their type of punch or kick.
Shinpo Matayoshi

During kumite, the most important part was hitting the other guy and also how you took getting hit. Everyone got hit. All these impressions presented a challenge and standard that drove me to work out harder.
Tom Muzila

In the old times the main purpose of the art was a self-defense, and was based on each individuals capability to adapt karate to his body structure, understanding, and knowledge. Karate was a highly efficient fighting tool that used the entire body as a weapon.
Tamas Weber

The dojos were very small and only one company sold uniforms. I remember when I got promoted, I had to wait six months for my black belt to arrive from Japan.
Val Mijailovic

Karate Wisdom

He trained under Funakoshi Gichin, but after few years Otsuka sensei began to move more into the kumite, or fighting aspect, and this approach was not shared by Funakoshi Sensei.
Yoshiaki Ajari

The idea of the art of Budo is to forget yourself and throw everything you have into practice. It is simple, there is nothing more to it. And some day you'll understand. It's something that has to be experienced, not told or explained.
Bill Dometrich

Mutual respect, courtesy, consideration, mutual welfare, honesty, integrity and openness are all desirable qualities for a good teacher. It is essential to develop these qualities and not just pay lip service to them.
Chuck Merriman

Japanese karate-ka will often work very hard to perfect their basic techniques without asking why the training is necessary, and will take quite a long term view of their training. They do not expect results in the short term.
Harry Cook

What I used to do, some say was brave, others foolish, but in fact it was an honored tradition known as dojo "yaburi." You fight against the lowest rank until you defeat the dojo's senpai. Then and only then, do you have

Tradition

the right to challenge the sensei himself. Probably, because of this practice, I became infamous and very good at kumite.
Teruo Hayashi

Training was very different them, it was more like an extended family arrangement, older brothers helping younger brothers. If you really stretch the point, all of them could say that they taught me. However, it's true that others would offer their advice from time to time even as I got older.
Morio Higaonna

There is something that has not changed during all these years and that is the mentality and the training spirit found in Master Funakoshi's dojo. This spirit is still inside of me.
Taiji Kase

Shito ryu, from my experience in other martial arts and karate styles, is a very systematic training program developed by my father and style founder Kenwa Mabuni.
Kenzo Mabuni

Funakoshi Sensei changed all the Okinawa kata to better fit into his conception of shotokan karate.
Takayuki Mikami

Sensei Funakoshi always kept a very strict discipline inside and outside the dojo. Karate-do was a way of life for him, not something to be left behind when you left the dojo.
Masatoshi Nakayama

Karate Wisdom

I recall that we had no dojo so we still rotated around the universities. Without a central dojo, things were no as smooth as they should have been.
Hidetaka Nishiyama

Master Funakoshi never said that we should copy his form because he understood that his body weight and his body-type made the stances and the form of the techniques that way. He was a very scientifically-minded person.
Teruyuki Okazaki

Karate, as practiced in Okinawa's Ryukyu kingdom, was never a coherent, structured system, and training methods varied greatly from teacher to teacher.
Patrick McCarthy

Nishiyama Sensei taught me to think and organize my thoughts—how to organize my life. I didn't have a hell of a lot in common with most people. I had a limited education so I wasn't going to sit down and discuss physics with anyone.
Ray Dalke

The testing for sandan is the most difficult of all grading; it's very dangerous. For the next six weeks all I did was train and worry! I was going to be the first gaijin testing for sandan. And I did pass the test.
Stan Schmidt

In the past the repetition and many hours of physical exercises were strenuous and there were dangerous implications to the training that hurt many students. However, the respect and courtesy were exceptional.
Tino Ceberano

TRADITION

The fundamental element of shotokan is that we try to be strict with ourselves because there is no limit to what we can accomplish. We must be straight and honest with ourselves. This is the tradition of Funakoshi Gichin.
Tsutomu Ohshima

Teruo Hayashi Soke had very loyal students. For this reason, politically and socially, the Hayashi-ha Shito-ryu Kai is very stable. Wisely, Soke allowed us the freedom to try different ways to become skilled at natural movement. As a result, our training methods change and even our katas change over time.
Akio Minakami

One day Ryuritsu Aragaki took me aside and said, "I can see that you have a great passion and desire to train in goju-ryu karate. You should train with the foremost authority on goju-ryu in Okinawa, Grandmaster Meitoku Yagi; he is the top, senior student of Chojun Miyagi."
Anthony Mirakian

My father had many students and some formed new groups, some of which are now gone. But my father agreed that they could start or go their own way.
Goshi Yamaguchi

The art of karate-do includes the element of self-development, and technical training is the first stage to achieve this.
Hajimu Takashima

I always admired and still do, the old Buddhist monks in old Japan. They were real human beings who did not believe in killing any kind of life. But if someone was coming for them, they turned into fierce fighters.
Jon Bluming

Karate Wisdom

Tani Sensei dedicated his life to karate more than any other karate-ka that I have ever known. Sensei used to think of karate all the time, and he had thought up new, unique ideas for the art, including the double-twist or kick-shock, which increases the power in the techniques.
Kunio Miyake

Tradition teaches not only etiquette but also the character development that is very important to me. The way of karate-do is applied to every aspect of one's life and this is Budo karate.
Koss Yokota

To achieve the most value from karate-do, it should form part of one's lifestyle. It should be a regular habit, not a seasonal pastime or recreation.
Malcolm Dorfman

Karate must be followed the way it is, and you cannot try to change it. When you get into your car to go to work, you follow the street, right? You don't create new streets or simply go ahead because you don't like curves! You follow the streets. That's the way karate is and the way it should be practiced.
Masahiko Tanaka

TRADITION

All forms of martial arts start with courtesy and respect. The main idea of Budo is to remove all arrogance and pomposity and replace them with humbleness and the right spirit.
Ryusho Sakagami

Educational karate promotes life-long pursuit of growth and enjoyment and is open to all, regardless of age or innate talent level.
Shojiro Koyama

Masters transfer the "purity" of the styles to the students who are strong spiritually and technically, because these students have the "strength" to continue the tradition.
Seinosuke Mitsuya

A good instructor should be hard and dedicated to what he does. At the same time, he has to be understanding to the student's needs and be there to help him when he needs it. This applies not only inside the dojo but outside as well. A good sensei in the traditional Budo concept is much more than a simple teacher of a fighting art.
Shigeru Sawabe

Karate Wisdom

Miyazato Sensei was Master Miyagi's senior student. When Miyagi Sensei died, Miyazato Sensei received all the training equipment and established his own dojo to continue the teachings of Master Miyagi.
Teruo Chinen

When the old masters designed the structure of the art, they did it in such a way that the changes were accommodated when the right time came in the practitioner's life. Instructors must understand this point and ensure that older students do the things in the right way and train within their own limitations.
Tatsuo Suzuki

Traditionally, the art was taught to the student in a tailor-made format. The teacher had the time and motivation to make the art or style fit perfectly with the student's physical make-up and qualities.
Yashunari Ishimi

Under Japanese Budo, one does not initially challenge the master of a particular school or style; a challenge is first issued to the senior student. If the challenger defeats the senior student, then he can challenge the master. If the challenger defeats the master, he can take the dojo sign as a trophy.
Yasuhiro Konishi

The correct understanding of karate and its proper use is karate-do. One who truly trains in this Do [way] and actually understands karate-do is never easily drawn into a fight.
Gichin Funakoshi

That karate has come to be identified in the public mind as an "art of homicide" is indeed sad and unfortunate. It is not that. It is an art of self-defense, but in order to attain its benefits, the practitioner must be completely free of any egotistic feeling.
Shigeru Egami

TRADITION

I personally derive great satisfaction from training and teaching karate, and most importantly from learning new concepts.
Alex Sternberg

Karate is more than a way to defend oneself or improve physical conditioning. it is a way of life and a way of improving one's life.
Eihachi Ota

Master Kenwa Mabuni taught shuri-te first in order to acquire basic fighting skills. Then he taught naha-te to develop power. So all other shito-ryu groups are shuri-te based and put naha-te on top of the shuri-te base.
Keiji Tomiyama

You didn't have three or four months to prepare your kata and sharpen your timing in kumite. The idea was that a real martial artist should be prepared at all times.
Kiyoshi Yamazaki

Tradition is based on a chain-of-command relationship. Each entity of this chain never questions the previous one because of the injection of morality from its predecessor. Consequently, over a period of some time, the product becomes quite stereotyped.
Mas Oyama

Budo is a vehicle for a deep transformation inside the human spirit.
Yoshinao Nanbu

Karate and martial arts are the result of many years of training, research and evolution. They contain cultivation and refinement, but unfortunately, instead of trying to preserve the heritage that our ancestors preserved for us.
Yuishi Negishi

Karate Wisdom

Early in our training with Mr. Ohshima, we were taught to defeat our strongest opponent—ourselves—and our fears and weaknesses. Karate aligned the very being of physical existence to face, harmonize and extinguish weaknesses.
Tom Muzila

The bottom line is that karate-do is a violent art. Because of the times of peace we are living in, however, a part of that art can be used as an enjoyable sport activity.
Tamas Weber

Mas Oyama really enjoyed things like bending coins, breaking bottles, and the famous fight with the bull. I saw him to do some very amusing things. I really can't tell you how much truth there was in every one of those things, but he was a very enjoyable person to be with.
Yoshiaki Ajari

In Budo, discouragement is part of the training, there is nothing wrong with being discouraged. The important point is not to misunderstand it and quit practice, but to keep training as usual. It takes times, but in the end you realize that there was no reason to be discouraged.
Bill Dometrich

TRADITION

Sensei Sakagami always told me that the original Okinawan kata were easier on the body, because they put less stress on the joints. I didn't appreciate the truth of this until years later.
Fumio Demura

The fundamental "raison d'etre" of the traditional teachings of karate is the development of effective fighting or self-defense skills. Ideas such as "zanshin," fighting spirit, tolerance to pain and minor injuries, et cetera are there to enhance your physical skills of kicking, punching, blocking, striking, throwing, and locking. Without such ideas there is no karate.
Harry Cook

As a teacher, I need to find better ways to communicate and pass the knowledge depending of whom I'm teaching at that time. Students have different backgrounds, education levels, understanding, et cetera and you have to adapt accordingly.
Teruo Hayashi

Karate Wisdom

Good karate makes good people, and I feel a responsibility to pass on what was given to me as a way of thanking my teacher, An'ichi Miyagi.
Morio Higaonna

Sensei Funakoshi was continually changing and improving the art. I would say that he liberated karate from the precepts of Okinawan karate.
Taiji Kase

As for as myself, I keep my father's traditions and teachings the way he taught them. It's my job to preserve his art and knowledge as purely as possible.
Kenzo Mabuni

The original stances were made for fighting but since the purpose no longer holds they adapted karate to the present day, looking for a better overall physical development.
Takayuki Mikami

Sensei Mabuni was a very respected karate-do master and Gichin Funakoshi had high respect for him. He was a living encyclopedia of kata from many different sources.
Masatoshi Nakayama

We didn't practice many techniques or combinations. No variety at all. One hour kiba-dachi, 1,000 punches, 1,000 kicks, and pretty much that was it!
Hidetaka Nishiyama

My generation was very fortunate to have trained under Funakoshi Sensei and to have been led by Nakayama Sensei, but I guess that no one considers themselves good enough to do the job we have to do. We

were educated to believe in high quality karate-do, both technically and spiritually.
Teruyuki Okazaki

Life at that time was very disciplined. Life, pre-war, was very, very strict. It was a time of rising Japanese militancy in people minds. I remember that both judo and kendo were part of the educational system for imparting the ways of the warrior to the young.
Osamu Ozawa

Karate is a microcosm of the austere culture from which it comes. Irrespective of its Chinese origins and early Okinawan cultivation, karate is a miniature representation of Japanese society. Karate-do reflects ancient rituals, inflexible social ideology, and profound spiritual conviction.
Patrick McCarthy

If your instructor is old and you are young, you are going to perform karate differently. However, students should listen to their instructor. The students must understand that they need to train their bodies in a different way. They need to listen more rather than copying their teachers.
Yasuhiro Konishi

As far as tradition goes, of course Japanese see things different than we do in the West. But that doesn't keep me from feeling that I've achieved whatever they think I was incapable of as a non-Japanese.
Ray Dalke

Don't forget that the rank always bring a big responsibility as well. The higher the rank you have, the higher the responsibility you accept.
Stan Schmidt

Karate Wisdom

Ritual exercise means nothing without the understanding and practice of courtesy and respect to the sensei and fellow students, including oneself.
Tino Ceberano

Karate is a way of life, maybe a little lower than what we understand as "religion," but it can used to achieve a higher level of mentality.
Tsutomu Ohshima

It would be inappropriate to ask further explanation without first trying. Students must accept instructor's modifications and then go home and work until they get the answers. After a few years of effort, if they must question, then they question.
Akio Minakami

The karate training consisted of a blending of physical, mental and spiritual elements harmonized in a very smooth way. There was no harshness. The grandmaster led the class in a strict and disciplined way, but he did it with a friendly attitude. The karate students felt very comfortable being taught by Grandmaster Meitoku Yagi.
Anthony Mirakian

In bushido, it's not how much you think about yourself. That's the most important point. You think about your boss and your country. That is the main idea.
Goshi Yamaguchi

You should do karate for the sake of karate, then the other things like self-defense and etiquette will follow.
James Yabe

TRADITION

I can write a book about Donn F. Draeger and my experiences with him. He was my real sensei since the first day when he picked me up and asked me to help him to prove a point in a class.
Jon Bluming

Karate-do is not only a method of fighting, but it's also a way of strengthening relationships between yourself and society.
Kunio Miyake

Bowing etiquette between the students and to the sensei are enforced and followed less. Such etiquette is a crucial part of Budo, so it is my opinion that we must never forget or ignore it.
Koss Yokota

The most important thing to keep in mind is that all forms of Budo are not courses of study, but rather, a way of life.
Ryusho Sakagami

Karate Wisdom

It is the instructor's responsibility to help the student appreciate karate as a lifetime art rather than always seeking a particular rank or a medal or trophy.
Shojiro Koyama

Each style represents a different flavor in the big landscape of the art of karate. A ryu (a style or system) is a method, and it is tradition, manners, philosophy, culture, science, technology, et cetera.
Seinosuke Mitsuya

It was Miyazato Sensei who gave birth to Jundokan. There is an old Chinese poem called Jundo Seisho. Translated, this means, "Do the right way." Miyazato Sensei took a quotation from it.
Teruo Chinen

Rank was never a relevant thing in Japan. In fact, rank is something that became popular in the Western world. Teachers in Japan don't go around bragging about their rank. It is something that only brings a bad reputation and proves how immature they are.
Tatsuo Suzuki

Shito-ryu has a strong influence from Okinawa's culture, and they [Okinawans] tried to make the practice of karate very natural for the human body. Karate is a part of the practitioner's life, and the Okinawans approach it like something that you will be doing for the rest of your life.
Yashunari Ishimi

Chojun Miyagi, by all accounts, did not talk very much. He was famous for his big hands, and he was noted for grabbing and pulling very strongly. Though my father did not train with Miyagi Sensei as much as with other karate masters, Miyagi Sensei did impact my

Tradition

father's knowledge of karate by presenting him with an original manuscript, "An Outline of Karate-Do," dated March 23, 1934.
Yasuhiro Konishi

Karate-do strives internally to train the mind to develop a clear conscience, enabling one to face the world honestly, while externally developing strength to the point where one may overcome even ferocious wild animals. Mind and technique become one in true karate.
Gichin Funakoshi

It must be kept in mind that Japan has a cultural tradition and educational background solidly etched in martial arts. Training attitudes are therefore very different, Young people are not surprised to have their mistakes corrected by being struck by a shinai.
Kiyoshi Yamazaki

There are many levels of the bow. An true sensei can watch ten different martial artists bow and immediately know what kind of mental and technical level each person has. He can see all of this in their form, breathing, eyes, state of mind and mannerisms.
Tom Muzila

Karate in its early days had no match rules, although there was a gentlemen's agreement to avoid attacking vital organs.
Masatoshi Nakayama

Grandmaster Meitoku Yagi felt that the emphasis in goju-ryu karate should be karate-do … karate as a way of life. He said that there was a spirit of Budo in karate that is different from the spirit of sports.
Anthony Mirakian

Karate Wisdom

The traditional styles were put together with a sense of balance. Everything in a particular style was designed and glued together with meaning and reason. The techniques, the strategies and the principles found in the forms, et cetera, [all] work perfectly together like the pieces of a puzzle.
Ryusho Sakagami

Styles are different methods of training and represent different answers to the same problems. All of these aspects are like a sort of genetic identity or a DNA.
Seinosuke Mitsuya

Chinese mind goes with the Tangtse and Hwan Rivers ... slowly but surely. Even conversations between Chinese people are a little mystic; they never reveal their entire mind.
Teruo Chinen

He who would study karate-do must always strive to be inwardly humble and outwardly gentle.
Gichin Funakoshi

We need more education and research in karate. We need everyone with experience to be included, not excluded, from the family of karate. Only if we do this will we grow as one.
Alex Sternberg

My teachers have constantly given me inspiration and motivation. I have formed ideas about karate should be and I try to implement it in myself. It is the main motivation for my own development.
Keiji Tomiyama

TRADITION

What is important is to understand and respect the changes and differences in the different ryu. By understanding those differences, we will always be able to remember our roots and at the same time appreciate what other styles have to offer.
Kiyoshi Yamazaki

Karate-do is something that can only spring from within. Because of that, you should inspect yourself as you would a weapon and notice your strong points and weaknesses. This internal journey will make you a better human being.
Yoshinao Nanbu

Preserving physical techniques is not a big deal, but preserving the right attitude takes a dedicated effort. This is our responsibility as leaders of the martial art of karate.
Yuishi Negishi

If a martial artist wears his belt tight around the waist, he likely does not understand correct breathing. After years of breathing practice, the lower abdomen will protrude slightly outward. The belt must go around the lower portion of the abdomen so it does not restrict breathing.
Tom Muzila

Karate Wisdom

Rank has nothing to do with the idea of learning. The higher your rank, the more time you have to dedicate to the art to reach higher levels of understanding.
Tamas Weber

Wado-ryu is a karate style that focuses on middle distance—we like to enter and crash inside. This is more safely done using your strong side. Structurally, it is a faster method than those using the strong-side in the back.
Yoshiaki Ajari

For Master Funakoshi, karate was not a sport but a way of life. He always advised us to practice and keep practicing all the time. In fact, the training we did then with swords was perfectly applicable to karate!
Taiji Kase

Master Funakoshi collected the kata of his forerunners and then systematized them into 15 kata for practice.
Masatoshi Nakayama

Sometimes I wonder how the old masters knew about the right physics and dynamics of the human body.
Hidetaka Nishiyama

Master Funakoshi's last years were taken up with instruction and preparation to send instructors all over the world.
Teruyuki Okazaki

Karate came out of people having to defend themselves with their empty hands against oppressors. In order to gain strength a lot of these peasants on the island of Okinawa may have gone to a spiritual leader for guidance.
Stan Schmidt

Tradition

A successful karate-ka must be able to engage, exchange, and enjoy his art and, most importantly, contribute or convey to his fellow man the understanding—coded by our practice of respect, courtesy and awareness to others—when called upon.
Tino Ceberano

My second goju-ryu karate master, Ryuritsu Arakaki, told me that if we take the morality, the ethics and the meditative aspects out of karate, we're left with only animal skills.
Anthony Mirakian

In Japan, bushido must be a way of a loyalty. The Japanese have the concept of giri, which is an obligation to loyalty.
Goshi Yamaguchi

Protocol and rituals have very little to do with the actual fighting, but they are vehicles to preserve education, politeness, etiquette, et cetera. All these are very important values for a student. The people who criticize this simply don't have the knowledge of what these aspects represent.
Ryusho Sakagami

Master Funakoshi spoke frequently about the importance of balance in all things. Mental, emotional, physical and spiritual balance are essential to pursue perfection of character, a principle underpinning in the art of karate.
Shojiro Koyama

Every style reflects the method, the correctness and the rectitude of the master who created it.
Seinosuke Mitsuya

Karate Wisdom

The Okinawan practitioners took the teachings and adapted it, giving it an Okinawan flavor and creating the birth of Okinawan karate.
Teruo Chinen

The concept of sempai-kohai is mostly misunderstood in the Western world and difficult to incorporate properly in a dojo when you teach outside Japan. For the Japanese, these kinds of things are natural. Outside of Japan, students don't understand it.
Tatsuo Suzuki

To truly understand the real value of traditional karate-do, the practitioner needs to spend years training in the proper way and under a competent instructor. It is only after years of practice and a certain level of maturity that an individual will be able to perceive all the benefits of Budo and not just stay on the surface of the physical movements.
Kiyoshi Yamazaki

Tradition

If you practice a kata in which you have to jump 360 degree in the air and land flat on your hands, are you planning to do that when you are 60? You have to be logical in your approach to karate. Using logic, you can practice the art for the rest of your life.
Yashunari Ishimi

The training in Okinawa is very different than Japan. The practitioners work by themselves and don't follow the militaristic structure used in Japan.
Shinpo Matayoshi

In Budo, the teacher teaches in circles. You have to "steal" the knowledge because the knowledge won't be given to you. You have to develop your own feeling and perception of everything surrounding you.
Yasuhiro Konishi

Everyone should try to read and educate themselves about the art of Budo.
Tamas Weber

Master Funakoshi was against tournaments but I remember Nakayama Sensei telling him that it was a good way to promote the art and introduce it to the public.
Teruyuki Okazaki

Karate-do evolved not only from our humble masters from Okinawa but also for many years outside of Japan. Today, it has developed into a major household word, and it's important in regards to physical education and cultural attributes.
Tino Ceberano

Karate Wisdom

The Okinawans are the true masters of the art and they have a deep knowledge and repertoire. Okinawans are humble, peace-loving people. Like the Chinese, they refrain from ostentatious display, wild claims and ego trips.
Anthony Mirakian

The word sensei has very different connotations and meanings that extend way beyond winning a tournament. There are no coaches or trainers in Budo.
Ryusho Sakagami

Generally, karate is a serious matter for Japanese; it is not simply a sport. Unfortunately, due to the differences in culture with the Western world, I often notice a certain lack of seriousness from the Westerners who are involved in the arts of Budo.
Seinosuke Mitsuya

People must pass on the traditions and not lose them.
Teruo Chinen

Ohtsuka Sensei told us that karate in not perfect and that if we see something good from other sports or another martial art we should add it to build up our karate technique. He did this himself when he formulated wado-ryu.
Tatsuo Suzuki

Don't expect miracles though, because the martial arts won't bring any kind of mystical powers! It is important that a martial art instructor foster a sense of self-responsibility on the part of his students.
Ryusho Sakagami

TRADITION

Students need to understand that what they are learning from the instructor is the foundation; they need to build the rest.
Yasuhiro Konishi

Only those with a higher ideal will find karate interesting enough to persevere in the rigors it entails.
Gichin Funakoshi

The basic difference between today's training and when I started is that today's training is easier. It's not as strict as it was in the past. If Mr. Funakoshi, Miyagi, Motobu or Mabuni sensei saw our training today, I think they would be shocked—truly and really shocked.
Kiyoshi Yamazaki

The principles of karate are based on the principles of life and the universe. It is the realization of an existing phenomenon—such as a punch or a kick—that gives meaning to that phenomenon, and it is the understanding of that meaning that allows one to master the phenomenon.
Ryusho Sakagami

The only way to understand every aspect of karate-do is through constant practice and dedication. As in any other activity, it is necessary to have professionalism and dignity.
Seinosuke Mitsuya

Training

修業

Karate Wisdom

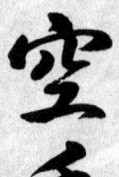

Practice kihon for the correct basics, kata for balance, coordination, and spirit, and kumite for an understanding of the application. There must be harmony between all three.
Alex Sternberg

You should not try to look like your teacher. The point is to understand the principles of karate technique and to adapt them to your own unique body and personality. Karate is an art and no two people should look the same.
Avi Rokah

A gyaku-tsuki hasn't changed because it can't change—it is the way the individual uses the technique that may change.
Dominique Valera

To me, karate training is something very individual and personal. I have had many students respond well to traditional training and enjoy the process—but I realize it is not for everyone.
Eihachi Ota

Find a good instructor. Someone who teaches Budo and not only sport. Someone who knows how to help the student grow and mature.
Tatsuo Suzuki

When doing kata you must live the form. Each kata must be done full-out. If done correctly, the karate-ka will reach his physical limits and not be able to continue. He'll be near his end. You shouldn't endlessly repeat a kata. To do so is to show that one is not living the kata.
Keinosuke Enoeda

Even now, I am correcting my technique. I must keep training. I want my skills to become better every day. I think I understand better now

Training

how techniques work, how the human body works. This has helped me to improve my skills and those of my students.
Hideharu Igaki

I don't believe that one system is good enough—none of them. No single one is fully adequate. Each system has good points. So what I teach combines everything. My fighting technique comes from my days with the university karate team.
Katsutaka Tanaka

As our techniques do not require great muscular strength or big dynamic movement to produce power, it is well suited to older practitioners who have started to reach limitations in their external power.
Keiji Tomiyama

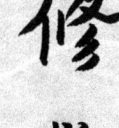

Kata and kumite should be divided 50-50. The karate-ka should balance his training because the path to perfection—a perfection that is never achieved, by the way—is based on balance.
Kiyoshi Yamazaki

Towards the end of my stay at the mountains, I got glimpses of what is meant by both "release" and the "thoughtless state." I gradually became capable of deepening mental unification until I moved from concentration to release and then to the thoughtless state of liberation—where I was able to foresee an opponent's motions and react to them at once without thinking.
Mas Oyama

I am always open to new things and new methods. This helps me to improve my karate. It is good to see that so many other karate-ka feel the same way.
Yukiyoshi Marutani

Karate Wisdom

The black belt-holder hasn't been born, no matter what their rank, who can block a bullet, or even jump away from one. That's why the martial art teacher has to be an impeccable example of integrity.
Yoshinao Nanbu

The art has evolved significantly, especially in the last 20 years or so. This evolution has affected the technical aspects of karate. We used to train short techniques such as kizami- tsuki or mae-ashi-geri because they were better for real fighting. Nowadays, since the emphases on karate's sportive aspects is bigger, the fighting distance is wider and most techniques are delivered by the rear hand and leg.
Yuishi Negishi

I work on the basics first and then I move on to kata and some fundamental exercises to maintain the necessary body coordination required to perform the techniques correctly.
Tatsuo Suzuki

The wado style is very subtle in the way it uses energy. You don't crash into the opponent, you use a lot of tai-sabaki to redirect your opponent's energy and find the right position. I truly believe that wado is a very good karate style for competition due to its mobility and practical approach to fighting.
Seiji Mishimura

TRAINING

Today's understanding of body mechanics is better, physical conditioning is better, and karate athletes are much more sophisticated in their movements, coordination, and agility.
Randall Hassell

Karate and kobudo have to be practiced by the body first, and followed by intellectualizing the action. You can explain how the body moves when you punch, but this doesn't mean you either know the technique or you are capable of using it against an opponent.
Shinpo Matayoshi

The most important and basic element is concentration. It is not simply a matter of going through the movements physically.
Tom Muzila

After some time of hard and dedicated training, my personal understanding and knowledge of the art increased very much. The kata, bunkai and kumite aspects became part of a complete new dimension, compared to my previous understanding.
Tamas Weber

Training has always been a passion for me. I look forward to what life has to offer. As I grow older things become clearer. Much like the farmer gets to know his land, I get to sense changes in my training.
Val Mijailovic

Karate Wisdom

There are many people out there with great amounts of physical talent for sports, but they don't work as hard as other less-talented athletes. In the end, the guy with all that talent will end up doing something else and the one who worked hard because he wasn't as gifted is the one who will be successful. Talent without hard training means absolutely nothing.
Wally Slocki

I often spent long periods of time staying at Mount Kurama where I subjected myself to ascetic exercises and hard physical training, especially training sanchin kata, meditating and enduring intense fasting.
Gogen Yamaguchi

Wado-ryu uses a lot of lateral and sidestepping maneuvers and goju-ryu bases its actions on short snapping techniques. They don't move the body around too much. Goju-ryu works in close distance and wado-ryu operates moves more in middle distance—similar to shito-ryu.
Yoshiaki Ajari

The training in the Western world and Japan also has undergone a great change over the past forty years. It is more technical now with much more kumite. Many years ago we did a great deal of kata and self-defense training and very little kumite.
Bill Dometrich

"Training," and "study," are completely different. Studying is much more than showing up for practice, just like studying in college is not just showing at the school and then sitting there. Study is a learning process which entails research about philosophy, technical aspects, physiology, and other related matters. It is much deeper than just training.
Chuck Merriman

Training

Like anyone else, my first years were cramming in all the training I could, jumping in with both feet, not really stopping to analyze techniques. Then, as the years went on, I begin to realize the dynamics and principles of proper kicking and striking. You learn that when something is executed the right way, you can cause more damage with your technique.
Dan Ivan

I don't recommend mixing styles. I tried to do it with shotokan and shito ryu and it just didn't work. There are a lot of reasons why many of today's modern innovators are going back to the traditional systems.
Fumio Demura

The syllabus of our group, the Seijinkai Karate-Do Association, makes use of techniques and kata drawn from both shotokan and goju ryu, and training methods derived from a wide range of systems which reflects both my background.
Harry Cook

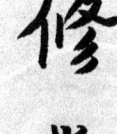

I train hard every day. I've seen very good martial artists that stopped training after the 40-year-old mark. The secret is to keep training hard. Of course, you're going to lose some speed and power in your technique but you can make it up with superior experience and knowledge about both the mental aspects and the real way the techniques work.
Teruo Hayashi

I don't practice tai chi for tai chi, but for my karate.
Hirokazu Kanazawa

When karate was developing there were many gaps to be filled. Master Funakoshi knew that the influence of other methods was essential and that's why I'm trying to incorporate them. I truly believe in a healthy karate.
Taiji Kase

Karate Wisdom

Zen training can greatly help your karate and in the end, help you in life. Real spiritual training is present in every moment of our lives. But don't forget that Zen training is not only done with your head, but also "with your flesh and bones," as the master said.
Kenei Mabuni

We used to do a lot of kihon—thousands of repetitions of each technique. Master Nakayama was a very tough instructor. The old training was very samurai-like. We used to drill, and drill, and drill without the instructors explaining anything.
Takayuki Mikami

The training under Funakoshi Sensei was very hard and demanding; the classes consisted of long hours of performing each technique hundred of times.
Masatoshi Nakayama

TRAINING

What it is true in any style is the fact that regardless of the style, every karate-ka needs to know how to develop power in short range and long range using strong muscle actions and contractions.
Hidetaka Nishiyama

We would stand in kiba-dachi and punch for two hours in the morning. Then the same for another two hours in the afternoon and for another two hours in the evening. Most people just gave up.
Teruyuki Okazaki

We did an hour of non-stop basics and then an hour of combinations then two hours of free sparring and then another hour of combinations. It was really brutal. You can't do that with the students today.
Ray Dalke

The training used to take place on the beach. It was more of a private training and you had to be recommended by at least two people. It was pure martial arts, and the conception of fighting was about life or death, not about winning tournaments.
Tsuguo Sakumoto

Sometimes senior practitioners don't understand that doing things in a very relaxed way is more beneficial that using the hard approach. After all, if you keep practicing a mistake you'll only get good at the mistake.
Stan Schmidt

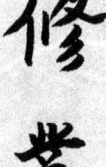

KARATE WISDOM

My training was very hard; everything evolved around number 500: 500 kicks, 500 punches, 500 stance changes, 500 hits to the makiwara, and 50 minutes of kata. Everyday was very much the same. My father was teaching me karate to fight to kill, not for self-improvement or sport but for war.
Takayuki Kubota

Regardless of how one chooses to look at it, it has always been the human body—its unique form, function, and common anatomical weaknesses—which have ultimately dictated which seizing and impacting techniques best impede an opponent's motor function, which is the dispassionate aim of self-defense.
Patrick McCarthy

Considerations of technical purity are measured on what indoctrination has implied ... believe what I say and not what I do. This is a way of saying that we know so much, but we must continue to pursue knowledge and progress with the times.
Tino Ceberano

I train differently than most people because of my Oriental medical background. You could say that I see everything from the standpoint of Ki in relation to the physical, mental and spiritual realms.
Tatsuo Hirano

The special training includes things like practicing at midnight, executing 1,000 techniques and/or holding a horse stance for 90 minutes. It is not easy, and that is why we call it special training. It's not ordinary, easy practice.
Tsutomu Ohshima

TRAINING

Be self-reliant. Karate training is for you and for nobody else. Make yourself strong and be smart. Avoid violence whenever possible but fight without fear if you must. In an emergency there is no one to rely on but you.
Akio Minakami

The training at Grandmaster Toguchi's school was intensive. We trained six days a week. The only day off was Monday. The training started at 6 p.m. and lasted until 10:30 p.m.
Anthony Mirakian

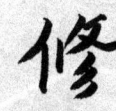

Basically, shotokan practitioners really seem to focus on just three things: The quality of our technique or our ability to make shock and focus with our techniques; our sense of timing and our use of distance.
Edmond Otis

I started karate at eight years old. At that time, we had no class for the children, so we trained with the adults, and the classes started late at night. What I remember most is that I could not eat supper if I didn't take class.
Goshi Yamaguchi

People are not so dedicated and willing to go through the hard training anymore. A new generation of student came along, a generation that couldn't be pushed in the 'old way.' I honestly think that we should go back to the old values and ethics.
H.Ohtsuka II

Otsuka Sensei trained in different styles and finally decided what was the best approach to combat. He developed a series of principles that should be used in combat, and his main idea was not to face strength with pure strength.
Hajimu Takashima

Karate Wisdom

When I went back to Japan in February 1959, I entered the Kodokan, where I met Peter Urban. He was from Yamaguchi Gogen's dojo, and he had big knuckles. So I started karate first with shotokan, but I found it weak.
Jon Bluming

My early days in karate were based on simple and pure kihon training. Only a few people stayed because there wasn't anything very interesting [going on]; repeating the same techniques thousands of times is not amusing to most practitioners.
Kunio Miyake

When I neared 50, I decided Ki may be the answer, so, in 1997, I moved back to Japan. I wanted to focus on Ki, so I gave up karate training for three years. I joined the famous Master Nishino's dojo in Tokyo.
Koss Yokota

The matches were so vicious that after [the referee yelled] "yame," the normally austere and serious instructors watching—including Tanaka Sensei, Yahara Sensei and Isaka Sensei—had huge grins on their faces. They loved it. The only problem was that I scored two points to his one, and my opponent never spoke to me for the remainder of my trip to Japan.
Malcolm Dorfman

TRAINING

I can say that all my karate power comes from those sprints during my rugby years because everything was ankles, knees and hips. Rugby helped to mold my legs in those early years.
Masahiko Tanaka

I want to teach my students so well that they are capable of winning any competition, and then I want them to travel worldwide. I also want people to know and learn my techniques and understand my aim for perfection.
Mikio Yahara

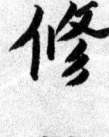

Funakoshi Sensei visited Mabuni Sensei, and he had some of his students learn kata from Mabuni Sensei. Later on, they modified things to better fit the style he was developing. Mabuni Sensei had a good relationship with Funakoshi Sensei.
Ryusho Sakagami

After a lifetime of experience, I understand that hardship and struggle must be incorporated—in the form of character development—into one's training in order to improve one's performance.
Shojiro Koyama

It is important to always improve. There is no end to that. It is necessary to coordinate your thoughts and actions, and you need to continuously practice hard every day and never give up.
Seinosuke Mitsuya

Karate Wisdom

Sakagami Sensei took me to Mabuni Sensei's dojo; that's how I met him. I continued studying karate-do with both Sakagami Sensei and Mabuni Sensei., Mabuni Sensei passed away. After that, I continued my training with Sakagami Sensei at his dojo. At that time, his dojo was located at his home.
Shigeru Sawabe

I was sent to Hawaii and Taiwan to teach the art. It was in Taiwan where I had the opportunity to meet several Chinese kung-fu masters with whom I shared training and knowledge. Some people approached me to learn and others challenged me, so I had to fight.
Tetsuhiko Asai

Miyagi Sensei group of students was comprised of different levels of skill, and he treated them according to their specific skill and understanding. He personalized the instruction for each student. This is the main reason why you see students of Miyagi Sensei doing the same things but slightly differently. He personalized the instruction and gave each student what he really needed at that period of time.
Teruo Chinen

The training was based on hard sessions of kihon and lots of sparring and fighting.
Tatsuo Suzuki

The training sessions were strict and demanding, including two special training per year; shochu-geiko in summer time and kan-geiko in winter. These training camps were extremely demanding for the body.
Yosuke Yamashita

Training

The "old" teacher used to send the student to a corner and ask him to repeat the movement 10,000 times. Then his questions would evaporate but I know this is not an acceptable way of teaching in the Western world. In the West, when a student asks you a question, you simply answer.
Yashunari Ishimi

The atmosphere at Takushoku was very competitive and that made everything more difficult and tougher than any other place. I really enjoyed my time there because there was a sense of honor in winning trophies and tournaments for your university.
Yoshiharu Osaka

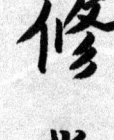

Karate is a technique that permits one to defend himself with his bare hands and fists without weapons.
Gichin Funakoshi

Karate should not be used indiscriminately.
Chotoku Kyan

In our physical movements, there are those that are natural and others that are not. Through the practice of karate-do, we can learn to differentiate between the two and also learn to acquire natural movements. We also learn of the power that nature endowed us with and how to use it, for a man has a great deal of hidden power of which he is not aware.
Shigeru Egami

The ultimate mastery of karate is being able to defend yourself by simply walking toward your opponent.
Takemasa Okuyama

Karate Wisdom

It's important to always understand what you are doing when you practice, how this gives more meaning to your skill, and how this will help to make you into a more effective fighter.
Alex Sternberg

Training was very rough when I first came, sometimes it felt like going to war. The senior students had some fresh meat to bite on. The first week that I came here, I got punched and had to get 24 stitches.
Avi Rokah

Sometimes when a practitioner is a gifted athlete, they actually achieve less because they do not have the work ethic or persistence. The right attitude is more important to a student than the natural ability to kick and punch.
Eihachi Ota

Only on certain occasion will one repeat a kata a number of times— and that is for mental and spiritual purposes—to force you to go beyond the body, the mind and the art. You have to live the kata. Use all your power as if in life or death.
Keinosuke Enoeda

I would urge karate-ka everywhere to always try to improve their skills. They should never be satisfied. They will help to keep karate strong if they are always trying to improve.
Hideharu Igaki

TRAINING

The human body has the ability to go beyond conventional limits of strength. When you feel like you can't go on anymore, that's when you really learn, that is when you really make progress. You are past that point and you no longer have to think about what you are doing.
Katsutaka Tanaka

The quality of your karate is determined by the quality of your basics, so you have to practice basics regularly and try to improve them whatever level you are at.
Keiji Tomiyama

Your karate-do should be technically balanced. If you can do good kata, but you cannot perform good kumite, then there is something wrong. And vice versa—being good at kumite but performing poorly at kata is a sign of unbalanced training.
Kiyoshi Yamazaki

Through Zen meditation the students concentrate on "mushin," which involves losing one's identity. The idea is clearing the mind so the student only concentrates on the training, allowing him to perform much better karate.
Mas Oyama

You work on your skills, your technique, your power. You begin to understand that you can handle the situation because you know that your technique is strong and it works. Then you are in control of the encounter, not the opponent. I want to emphasize the need for realistic kihon as applied to sparring.
Yukiyoshi Marutani

Karate Wisdom

Training has to be balanced. Real fighting is very different from point fighting or sport competition, not only in physical techniques but also how both situations are approached mentally.
Yuishi Negishi

The idea of training was to take the human body and turn it into a lethal weapon. You had to develop your fists, feet, elbows, knees, et cetera to the point they became a deadly tool of survival.
Seiji Mishimura

At my age, my job is to become more skillful and, therefore, less vulnerable to injury.
Randall Hassell

In the art of bujutsu and Budo, the difference between one whose mind wanders and the student who is attentive is much more apparent than any other field. Not only will the inattentive student get low marks, but they are more likely to have their bones broken when a kumite occurs.
Shinpo Matayoshi

You must control your mind so it is behind each and every single technique you perform. You can't let the physical or external stimulus be in control of what you are doing.
Tom Muzila

Karate was too dangerous to be taught to everyone because it could easily be misused. This is why it was necessary to frame the training with a code of values, honor, humility and respect.
Tamas Weber

I always liked the natural way of training. Running, sit-ups, and push-ups. During high school I tried weightlifting, but it did not work for

me. When I lift weights my body tightens up too much and it slows me down.
Val Mijailovic

The West has caught up and surpassed Japanese karate with regard to physical aspects, but they still have a long way to go to equal the philosophy and history of Japanese karate. The meaning behind it, the attitude toward the art, and the philosophical approach is still superior to the West.
Wally Slocki

The understanding of one's own body is crucial to the correct execution of the techniques, but today we have lost understanding of how our bodies work because of our daily chores and responsibilities. We have too many devices to do physical work for us.
Gogen Yamaguchi

The jiu-jitsu influence is not as obvious in the external movements but you can see it in the application and bunkai of the kata. It's here when we can see all the subtle details of locking and throwing from his jiu-jitsu training.
Yoshiaki Ajari

I was by no means a gifted karate student, although I learned the basics fairly easily. I had a very hard time, however, of getting the movements to flow and in the development of kime. Over years of training I slowly developed the ability to develop more power and better movement.
Bill Dometrich

In order to be a complete karate-ka you need to strike a balance between both, since one doesn't exist without the other.
Chuck Merriman

Karate Wisdom

Purists in the martial arts, especially karate, are rare and becoming almost extinct. Influences today change the way we teach, and what we teach; however, there are still a handful of sensei that flow with the times and still manage to maintain the true art with the right spirit and attitude.
Dan Ivan

You can't have a strong house without a strong foundation. The stronger the basics, the stronger the house—it's as simple as that. Unfortunately a lot of practitioners don't understand.
Fumio Demura

I also became very aware of the importance of conditioning and developing the ability to hit hard with single punches and kicks. This in turn led me to training with equipment. I have said many times that is fundamentally more efficient, and better for the body, to train your striking techniques by hitting a target such as a kick bag, makiwara, focus pads, et cetera, rather than performing endless repetitions into thin air, which in the long run is damaging to the joints.
Harry Cook

Your body changes and your karate changes with your body. You become softer as you grow older. Some young practitioners don't understand that everybody's karate has to be different, must be different, as the karate-ka gets older.
Teruo Hayashi

TRAINING

These days I see too much tension in the practitioners. They become so excited that they forget to relax their muscles. Trying hard is all they do and by the time they develop speed, their muscles are too tense.
Taiji Kase

There are changes and alterations to training methods according to the ages of practitioners and the instructor's applications. It's important to understand your own body so you can adapt your private training to that.
Kenzo Mabuni

Shotokan is a great style but it is very difficult for older people. It is important to find ways of adapting the methods without losing the principles.
Takayuki Mikami

Every karate practitioner has a different body. Through training and understanding kata in the right way, they seek their final form— they become their own masters for expressing karate. The principles are there and they come out naturally.
Hidetaka Nishiyama

Master Nakayama wanted us to train under other karate masters, that's why he used to invite Gogen Yamaguchi from goju-kai and Hinori Otshuka from wado-ryu to teach us a different approach to the art.
Teruyuki Okazaki

KARATE WISDOM

The more understanding you have about what you are doing, the less you need to change or modify. I do traditional kata, not personal kata. We shouldn't be changing kata to make it look more attractive in order to win points in a competition.
Tsuguo Sakumoto

You can hit me anywhere you want, and it will probably hurt you more than it does me. The program prepares you to take on anything.
Takayuki Kubota

I find most Westerners are deeply moved and affected by the depths of Japanese traditional culture in general and Budo in particular. Many have become not only great students but great masters and teachers as well.
Tatsuo Hirano

Although the karate students were not allowed to change the basic techniques, there was more flexibility than in other dojo. A tall student, for instance, wouldn't be required to go so deep into kiba-dachi or zenkutsu-dachi that he lost mobility.
Anthony Mirakian

My father liked to use Shinto in all aspects of his training, but he didn't say that everybody must do that, because this [Shinto] is a religion. He believed everyone had a right to his own religion, so he never told anyone he had to do it.
Goshi Yamaguchi

I was Oyama Sensei's first foreign student and stayed with him—the first time—for almost three years in the old dojo behind Rikyu University.
Jon Bluming

TRAINING

If you wish to compare or examine the technique and methodology of a certain ryu, you need to go to the source, which means you go to the headquarters or the original master.
Koss Yokota

Today, the training in Japan does not have the same harshness and intensity. That is detrimental for Budo, but it is certainly more conducive for the regular Western karate-ka to train there.
Malcolm Dorfman

I was a san-dan at the time, and I really wanted to take the courses for kenshusei [student instructor] at the JKA Headquarters. They refused my request because there weren't enough funds to support a student instructor at the time. However, if I could support myself, they said that I would be allowed to enter the course. Of course, I started to look for any kind of job that would allow me to pay my bills, and it didn't matter to me what kind of work it was.
Masahiko Tanaka

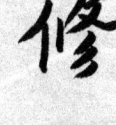

To make their training and life more productive, new generations should study all of the information they have today. With that, they should be able to go farther than we old teachers did.
Ryusho Sakagami

Technique comes from the instructor's personality and personal philosophy.
Shojiro Koyama

In order to practice karate properly, you need to learn how to relax the muscles and use them properly to generate speed. If your muscles are not relaxed, they simply can't be fast and you can't produce power.
Tetsuhiko Asai

Karate Wisdom

I have heard really silly stories about Miyagi Sensei, such as the one that he could leave his footprints on the dojo ceiling because of his ability to do a back flip so high that he kicked the ceiling. To begin with, the dojo was outside. It didn't have a ceiling! Miyagi Sensei was way too intelligent to risk damaging his body that way.
Teruo Chinen

The American government prohibited all kinds of martial training, including judo and kendo and most practitioners stopped their training at that very same moment, but there were some clubs where you could train because they managed to keep them open under the name of "Japanese boxing."
Tatsuo Suzuki

My father considered Choki Motobu to be a martial arts genius and made every effort to train with him. Motobu Sensei's specialty was the naifanchin kata. As a teacher, he knew many kata, but he would only teach them when his student had mastered naifanchin.
Yasuhiro Konishi

Once you have been taught the correct body mechanics and physical elements of a technique, you'll see that those are relevant to how the human body moves and they have nothing to do with the color of your skin or your genetics.
Yoshiharu Osaka

TRAINING

Once you have been taught the correct body mechanics and physical elements of a technique, you'll see that those are relevant to how the human body moves and they have nothing to do with the color of your skin or your genetics.
Yoshiharu Osaka

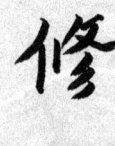

My impression was that Grandmaster Yagi felt that excessive weight lifting would cause flexibility and speed loss. He stressed that punching against the makiwara was the best way to develop devastating power.
Anthony Mirakian

Mas Oyama was like a father to me. He never let me pay for anything and always helped me out when I was low on money. He was a terrific teacher and really could raise my spirit when I felt really low. He also could put the fear of God into his students when they did not train the way he wanted them to train. It was the best years in my life.
Jon Bluming

Kata and kumite should not be considered as two separate and non-related components. They are two sides of a same coin, so to speak.
Koss Yokota

My personal shotokan developed into a very precise and technically orientated form of karate, far removed from the youthful version in which technical flaws were at times overlooked to ensure success at kumite.
Malcolm Dorfman

Karate Wisdom

In the JKA, we worked hard to develop a form of karate that uses the human body in the best possible way when it comes to utilizing all muscles and joints in the body to generate power. It is a very simple concept, but it is a difficult task to achieve.
Masahiko Tanaka

In doing a martial art, the mind, spirit and technique should all be fully expressed. If your technique is correct and your mind and spirit fully expressed and arrived, you will progress very fast.
Ryusho Sakagami

My philosophy is that karate is a lifetime exercise, and therefore, the instructor, as he ages, must continue to train his own mind and body.
Shojiro Koyama

It is necessary to know how to relax the muscles and use the natural energy of your body. Karate is good for health, so students need to find out how to do it right.
Tetsuhiko Asai

Miyagi Sensei was not in a good health, so he sat down a lot and directed the classes. He observed and gave instruction. We did a lot of kata. Kata and supplementary training were the basics of the training. The supplementary training included the makiwara, chiisi (stone lever weight), nigiri-game (gripping jars) and many other traditional items.
Teruo Chinen

The training at the university was very hard, and the instructors didn't care if the students quit because there were another 100 students waiting to enter the next month. This is the reason why the university had great fighters with a strong spirit and fearless determination.
Tatsuo Suzuki

Training

Correct technique is the result of a natural movement. If the technique is correctly practiced, the actions are harmonious, relaxed and powerful.
Yoshiharu Osaka

Most people who teach many different styles are actually not masters of any art, though they may make a lot of money at it, and they are certainly not masters of several arts. Most serious people, when they see a business card with a listing of many arts the person has supposedly mastered, dismiss that person as a braggart.
Alex Sternberg

Our style of karate is much more than athletic activity—it has unlimited personal growth potential. Behind our style there is knowledge accumulated through many generations—knowledge of both movement and the human being as a whole.
Avi Rokah

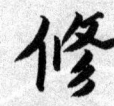

As a practitioner spends more time training, it is natural that the techniques and delivery systems evolve—if for no other reason than age, injuries, physical condition, et cetera. This will affect the way a practitioner executes and thinks about kata as well.
Eihachi Ota

In Budo karate-do, not sport karate, one must know and develop all these techniques—not just two or three. The way to avoid this is intensive kata training.
Keinosuke Enoeda

Breaking in my style is a way of testing our progress. It takes a lot of concentration and inner power because you can't only use your arm or leg. The power comes from the hara and it takes a minimum of ten years to develop the correct technique to use hara in breaking.
Mas Oyama

Karate Wisdom

I enjoy doing basics more and more every day—horse stance, footwork, hit the makiwara, combinations—and I enjoy sparring with the students.
Yukiyoshi Marutani

In a way, my personal training is a great fight between the inner part of myself and the natural aging process. It's a challenge between my body and my spirit. Time will tell who is the winner!
Tamas Weber

There is one area that the Japanese might have an edge—the college years. In Japan, karate is part of the curriculum at most colleges and universities. A young man can train every day, two to four hours, for his entire four years in school. So, for the 18 to 22-year-olds it is an advantage because you won't find many schools that keep up this regimen.
Dan Ivan

When I am training by myself I rarely perform techniques in the air, except of course when I practice kata. I would much rather hit something, even if it is just a piece of plastic foam hanging on a string.
Harry Cook

The practice was done very seriously, with tremendous concentration; the mind wasn't wandering, and there was no wavering of the eyes. Once the student was training in the dojo, he had to be in command of his mind and in complete control of himself.
Anthony Mirakian

Training

In November 1959, the President of the Kodokan called me into his office while Draeger translated. He told me that I had been chosen to join the kenshusei, a class in which the 25 best judo-ka from Japan all got together in a special class. I was very honored, and who was the head teacher? Mifune Sensei!
Jon Bluming

Train every day, but keep the practice segments short so your interest stays high for a long time. It is like boiling water and keeping it hot. You need a lot of heat initially to boil some water. Once the water is at the boiling temperature, you can keep it boiling with much less heat.
Koss Yokota

Karate training will improve anybody who trains correctly.
Malcolm Dorfman

JKA Shotokan is a straight down-the-line karate that places emphasis on good form, speed and kime. Is not that what any karate should be? JKA Shotokan is more a method or approach to karate than a separate style. Unfortunately, many people don't understand this.
Masahiko Tanaka

It is too easy to look for magic while the real secret is sweat. There is no magic in the martial arts, just a good teacher and a lot of hard work. The key is to practice, and I have always been an advocate for teaching the students everything I know. Holding back just weakens the art.
Ryusho Sakagami

Karate Wisdom

I don't really think about real fighting, and I believe that one should keep one's mind clear of thoughts about real-life enemies and fighting when training.
Shojiro Koyama

Unfortunately, many instructors around the world never learnt the right way and always practiced with tension and hard movements. This is one of the reasons why people think karate is a hard style while the truth is that it is not.
Tetsuhiko Asai

We simply cared about karate. We didn't need a belt to know who was good and who wasn't. Belt ranking came later, and it originated from the art of judo. They were using only three belts: white, brown and black.
Teruo Chinen

I was at Nihon University, and we had a pretty decent group of students. Unfortunately, the training was so hard that the attendance dwindled from 200 to 20. The rest simply decided it was too hard.
Tatsuo Suzuki

We need to study and develop methods for applications based on our own bodies and levels of understanding.
Yoshiharu Osaka

To mix styles just to mix them is not necessary or beneficial from my point of view. I do not believe that one style is superior to another, rather it is the individual who makes the difference.
Eihachi Ota

Training

There is no way an individual can learn the techniques, ethics and right attitude of karate without the guidance of an authentic instructor.
Mas Oyama

You can't lie to yourself. All psychological conditions are not the same in sparring as in a real situation, where panic and stress are at a very different level. But it is true that free-fighting is the closest to a real fighting situation you can come to in the dojo.
Tamas Weber

Lot of basics and sparring techniques are probably first, then kata, and then sport techniques for those in the class that attend sport tournaments. Kata should take up about a third, or maybe only a fourth of the training; the rest should be kumite, basics, and self-defense.
Dan Ivan

As far as I am concerned weight training of some kind is absolutely necessary if you want to improve your power levels. Power is a combination of speed and strength. Correct technique will give you the required speed, and when you add muscular strength the result is power. I have seen many modern karate-ka with excellent form but poor power levels—as far as I am concerned their training methodology is lacking something vital.
Harry Cook

You have to relax both your body and mind to detect changes in your opponent. Kake-uke was originally used to pair highly skilled practitioners for kumite. If one student could not move the arm of another student in kake-uke or could not hold his stance, he would not be allowed to engage in kumite with that student.
Anthony Mirakian

Karate Wisdom

I remember that Draeger Sensei took me to the Ueshiba dojo for aikido classes. I looked on in amazement. The movements were very nice, but on the street nobody is going to run around you and jump all over himself when taken by the wrist!
Jon Bluming

Hard training is important. You have to put your mind into it. Strive to find a good instructor; learn the right technique, timing, kime and the proper use of the body; and use your natural energy.
Tetsuhiko Asai

Okinawans follow the Chinese way more. They have a 24-hours martial arts mind. When they feel like training, they just do it. They don't care about the time. The Chinese are more relaxed about it.
Teruo Chinen

Starting one's training in a proper dojo is a must. If a student learns poor or wrong technique, it will be very difficult to correct or unlearn them later.
Koss Yokota

Technically, today's karate-ka are superior, but, in general, they lack the spirit of the samurai and the willingness to absorb physical pain to achieve the goal of being a Budo karate-ka.
Malcolm Dorfman

You can greatly improve your ability in sparring and self-defense by teaching yourself to observe clearly.
Masahiro Okada

TRAINING

The traditional training method of doing a high number of repetitions for kihon techniques is boring for the new generations. They don't want to repeat the same punch or kick 1,000 times. You can't treat the new students the way we were taught in the past.
Masahiko Tanaka

The reason that techniques are lost is not because the teacher withholds the knowledge. Instead, it's because today's students don't work to understand what lies behind the physical movements.
Ryusho Sakagami

All of the different styles are beautiful in their own right. That being said, I think of mixing karate styles much as I would of mixing different cuisines and cooking styles.
Shojiro Koyama

In Okinawa, the training is more individualized and personalized. Of course, the teacher corrects your mistakes, but the class structure follows the Chinese example in which students work on their own.
Teruo Chinen

Women are not built like men, so they use more technique and more subtle ways of doing the movements instead of relying on muscle and strength.
Tetsuhiko Asai

Karate Wisdom

At that time, you could easily recognize the practitioner's style because of his style of fighting. For example, the goju people in neko-ashi-dachi, the shotokan practitioners using a long distance approach, et cetera. Our [wado-ryu] style was something in between, but we used a lot of tai-sabaki and body evasion techniques.
Tatsuo Suzuki

Immediately after the war the training was not that strong because of the moral state of the people. Later on, however, we caught up and there were excellent training days.
Tatsuo Suzuki

Our body changes, sometimes due to injuries incurred during our younger training days. Therefore, the way we do our personal training has to adapt to these special circumstances. It would be stupid trying to do the same kind of training when you are 50 years old that you did when you were 25. That's Budo; that's why karate-do is a way of life.
Alex Sternberg

Our karate is about more than efficient use, it is about self-mastery— an endless journey that we will never reach. We are never going to be perfect but we can always get better.
Avi Rokah

Things like makiwara training and full contact sparring is practiced outside regular class and is a matter of individual choice.
Eihachi Ota

Don't focus excessively on sparring before a tournament; train kata. Then immediately before the tournament, move to one-step kumite, and then just few days before the tournament day, concentrate on free-sparring.
Keinosuke Enoeda

Training

Many of us got broken noses and teeth because of the free-sparring sessions everyday. We all felt some kind of fear as the free sparring session approached. Having once started fighting, you are too busy dealing with the job at hand and have no time to feel fear.
Keiji Tomiyama

Adapting teaching methods can greatly aid the development of the student. If you practice seriously, your body will know the techniques. If something happens, your body will react automatically—proper practice is the most important thing to remember.
Kiyoshi Yamazaki

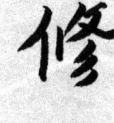

The essence of powerful and graceful movement and action in karate is balance, control, and coordinated effort. The body learns to immediately and accurately respond to the physical demands of the situation.
Mas Oyama

Power in karate should be developed through a consistent and dedicated approach to technique.
Seiji Mishimura

The real goal of this training is not the physical part—it is concentration—concentration in every single technique. It is a vehicle to improve your mental concentration, not just grunt endurance.
Tom Muzila

Endless training is good, but rational training is much better and will help to reach higher goals in the art and in the sport as well. Karate is a lifetime commitment. It is not something to be done for a few years and then quit, like they do in the universities in Japan or in the Western world after getting the rank of black belt.
Tamas Weber

Karate Wisdom

There are a lot of important values that are being overlooked by practitioners these days. If this is anybody's fault, it is the fault of the instructors.
Wally Slocki

I never adapted yoga breathing methods to karate. There are similarities and, of course, masters of karate and masters of yoga came to the same conclusions as far as the right breathing methods are concerned.
Gogen Yamaguchi

If you try to combine two or three styles you really need to know those methods and have a high level of understanding of how they work. Learning multiple martial arts styles or karate methods can become an obstacle to reaching a high skill level of mastery.
Yoshiaki Ajari

My techniques now look softer than they did years ago but they are really more powerful. I have come to realize that a great many of the techniques which impressed me when I started, no longer do so. I now realize that some of the most effective techniques are not that impressive looking nor photogenic.
Bill Dometrich

Authentic, traditional karate hasn't changed—just the people in it and their perception of what karate really is!
Chuck Merriman

TRAINING

Your lifestyle, age, and available time will dictate how much you'll be able to do. A mistake many people make is that because they can't do what they did before, they drop out. This is not wise. The practitioner has to make adjustments and do the best they can.
Dan Ivan

When we are young we try to show how tough we are and we do a lot of kumite. When we get older and our body starts to hurt, then we start to appreciate kata.
Fumio Demura

All karate methods were created by modifying, adapting and changing older models. This is the real tradition of karate's evolution, and different styles or "ryu" are only important in the sense that a ryu reflects one instructor's approach, or possibly a group of instructors. You should not expect any ryu to be passed on unchanged.
Harry Cook

For an older and more experienced karate-ka the time for the right kime in shorter. Some techniques can be very effective for young people, but they are impossible for an older practitioner to make work.
Teruo Hayashi

The shotokai style seems strange to anyone practicing the more orthodox systems of karate-do. The kata are the same as shotokan but are performed in a soft, slow and fluid fashion, reminiscent of tai chi. Egami Sensei was one of the senior students of Master Funakoshi and he was an excellent technician.
Taiji Kase

Karate Wisdom

Every practitioner should practice diligently and should neither copy other people nor other styles. It is important that one must personally practice techniques through their own physical exercise and gain experience through their own diligent efforts.
Kenzo Mabuni

Unfortunately, power and speed in techniques is over-emphasized and a lot of karate techniques do not need that much power or speed.
Takayuki Mikami

Kata was repeated 50 or 60 times and makiwara training was done until our hands bled. Master Funakoshi used to join us for makiwara training and hit the post with his elbow thousands of times. He seemed to enjoy that particular aspect of training.
Masatoshi Nakayama

I think that you have to relate so the students can understand. It's important that they realize that kihon, kata, and bunkai are just training methods like in football where they hit the pads or run sprints or run routes.
Ray Dalke

My training in the past 10 years has delivered the fruits of my labor, and I now see Ki radically different from before.
Tatsuo Hirano

The martial arts are not something you can copy. You must learn what lies behind the technique. The martial arts are taught today only like a good physical exercise. Unfortunately, they are lacking the true Budo spirit. The training is not geared to a real life-or-death situation, and this single fact changes the whole approach.
Ryusho Sakagami

TRAINING

Sanchin is the kihon kata, the basic kata, of Okinawan Goju-ryu. It has many purposes.
Anthony Mirakian

Physically, a Japanese person is much more flexible than the average European or American. In a way, that should be an advantage. In reality, it is not and the overall mental ability of the Europeans and Americans is much stronger than the average Japanese. That's a hardcore problem, but I believe that the average Japanese does practice much harder that the Westerner does.
Jon Bluming

A karate practitioner must perform karate techniques and use particular muscles in certain methods to produce power and movements. By just making some muscles stronger, it will not necessarily make your karate technique more powerful. Moreover, your karate technique may suffer.
Koss Yokota

The balance of hard and soft gives an understanding of human nature and creates a compassionate human being. Age limits physical prowess, but with the correct approach to karate training, the opposite applies with respect to wisdom.
Malcolm Dorfman

Hard, challenging training helps cultivate modesty and humility, which naturally leads to a better understanding of the spiritual aspects of the martial arts. Therefore, keep training, don't give up and don't become discouraged by your moments of weakness. Instead, learn to value and cherish them for the ultimate spiritual growth that they will bring you.
Shojiro Koyama

Karate Wisdom

If you don't put yourself at your very limit, how do you know how far can you go? How do you know how strong you are and how far your spirit will take you?
Masahiko Tanaka

Students must learn the basic body mechanics and form by punching and kicking in the air. This is simply the first step. It is at this stage in which the instructor should correct the technical mistakes. Students need to learn the proper use of the body, muscles and joints to generate power. Once the student has this skill down, impact training should be included. The body reacts completely different when you punch or kick a heavy bag or focus mitt compared to when you perform the technique in the air.
Tatsuo Suzuki

When a sensei arrives at a high technical level, he must emphasize the coordination between the mental and physical because this is an important aspect of the whole picture.
Seinosuke Mitsuya

Making the muscles tense is not good for your body and can cause many injuries during training. I want the students to learn and understand how to use the body properly and how to produce the right kime without using useless movements or unnecessary tension.
Tetsuhiko Asai

TRAINING

The training of the Ki is the training of the principles behind the moves. This involves the study of how the principles are used to give the correct energy application and the flow of the energy throughout the sequence of the moves.
Teruo Chinen

Only after exhaustion, pain, and even boredom does the body begin to perform what the mind cannot.
Joko Ninomiya

I trained very simply, but I did thousands of repetitions of the same movement. I also did a lot of makiwara, which I consider to be a very good training tool.
Tatsuo Suzuki

The natural body instinct slows down with age, but you have to keep training to revert this process back as much as you can. Train to develop focus and muscle control. These elements will be present during all of your years of karate, regardless of your age.
Yoshiharu Osaka

Those of us who are adhering strictly to orthodox karate as an art of self-defense must do all in our power to see that it is practiced in the proper way and that its spiritual side is understood to the fullest extent.
Shigeru Egami

Sensei Nishiyama's teaching is based on experience and intelligent methods of training rather than someone's dreams.
Avi Rokah

Karate Wisdom

Going to Okinawa or Japan to learn the art is no longer necessary these days. Trips overseas can be very beneficial and students are always welcome to join me when I travel to Okinawa. However, it is not necessary in order to achieve the highest levels of proficiency.
Eihachi Ota

Fear is an important part of the training of karate-do, but you should control this emotion and use it properly for your own benefit. Sometimes fear is a great thing because it forces you to be prepared for whatever may come.
Kiyoshi Yamazaki

There are different levels in karate. There is a physical level, a mental level and a spiritual level. Some people say there is only a physical level, simply because they only work the body.
Mas Oyama

To develop your mind and body you have to sweat. The school is not joining the student, the student is joining the school. I try to teach like this is a church, and people who join have to make a different kind of donation.
Yukiyoshi Marutani

Don't substitute your technical karate training for running or lifting weights because you will be making a mistake. You must first develop a strong technical foundation before you consider spending time in other physical conditioning aspects.
Yuishi Negishi

Only when your body mechanics are close to perfect should you gradually begin to incorporate the heavy bag. Too much heavy bag training will make your technique sloppy, so be careful. Try to add more power

TRAINING

without jeopardizing your technique. I have seen a lot of practitioners who had a very clean technique, become extremely sloppy and as soon as they started to punch the heavy bag.
Seiji Mishimura

Remember, in martial arts your center of gravity is just below your navel. You do not want to be top heavy and acquire a lot of shoulder power.
Tom Muzila

To me, goju-ryu karate and yoga are complementary to each other. By practicing karate, you improve your yoga breathing and by practicing yoga you help your karate technique.
Gogen Yamaguchi

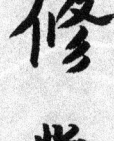

Karate teaches you more than fighting and combat. It teaches you discipline—both mentally and physically. Through the physical training of pushing your body to do things in a well coordinated way, you learn how to apply the force that lies inside your body in a very natural way.
Yoshiaki Ajari

Fear is part of Budo training. Feeling fear is irrelevant, what is important is how you control, re-direct and use this fear to overcome difficulties.
Bill Dometrich

Karate doesn't change, we do. I don't think it's a case of "has to change," but being aware of the natural process of physical and mental changes normally associated with aging. If you want longevity in your karate life, then the training in your younger years should be geared toward enhancing your ability to train in your later years.
Chuck Merriman

Karate Wisdom

Karate differs from all other activities because you should always be working against yourself, not others; so if you slow down or stop, you will find it harder to continue again.
Dan Ivan

It is not necessarily the amount of training that is important, but the type and quality of the training which is critical. Trying to perform techniques at the age of 60, as if you were 20 years old, is foolish.
Harry Cook

I try to steer clear of that "mysterious" approach to karate training. The real skills come from correct training methods, strong conditioning and endless repetition. Too many stories have been around the art for too long.
Teruo Hayashi

There is a point in every karate practitioner's life where the punch's unifying force must no longer be rooted in the muscles but in the internal organs.
Hirokazu Kanazawa

Don't forget about striking a balance in training between kata and kumite because that is the real secret.
Taiji Kase

TRAINING

Relaxation is very important in the art. Until you really understand how it works, and how beneficial it is for your body and technique, your training will be limited. The soft aspect is the other half of the equation.
Kenzo Mabuni

The good karate master teaches his students to find their own way, not to follow his. Students that venture out on their own too soon, or without the right amount of knowledge and understanding, will never know what they're doing.
Hidetaka Nishiyama

The basics are the same because we are human beings but the mental attitude has changed. Students think that if they pay this much, they must get that much. That's what they believe. The youth don't practice how to think.
Teruyuki Okazaki

I underwent their training and I broke my body and I wouldn't have been the person I am now if I didn't. Be careful because I don't just credit them for it I also credit myself for hanging in there.
Ray Dalke

You must teach your body to change and perform the technique under the perfect form principles based on physiology and body dynamics. You should learn to control your body movements and create the right technique for it according to the fundamental principles of physics.
Tsuguo Sakumoto

Karate Wisdom

It's only after at least ten years of training, when a student's body has absorbed the techniques, and the mind is free to work instinctively on fighting, rather than thinking about every move that you can really be a karate fighter. It takes ten years to produce a mature karate student.
Takayuki Kubota

I don't believe that the Japanese have any physical or fundamental differences or advantages … unless being smaller is an attribute. However, I do believe their work ethics are stronger and their training schedule certainly reflects this.
Tatsuo Hirano

When I started the special training in 1959, it was very experimental. People did have trouble adapting to the physical discipline. But all the tough guys wanted to take on this crazy Japanese guy and prove that they weren't chicken. I challenged them to show me how strong they were, and they ended up adjusting very well to the demands of the training.
Tsutomu Ohshima

At Grandmaster Kanryo Higaonna's dojo, the students performed nothing but sanchin and basic techniques for the first three to four years of training.
Anthony Mirakian

As the karate-ka gets older, and after about 30 or 40 years of practice in one art, he will benefit greatly from supplementing his training with a softer art such as yoga or even tai chi.
Shojiro Koyama

Although it is stereotyped as a "hard style," the best shotokan stylists understand the fundamental principles of the system in a way that lets them be fluid and soft whenever they are not hitting their target.
Edmond Otis

Training

Yoga is good for your breathing, and this comes in handy when you are working on your breathing. In the goju classes, my father taught the students how to do breathe properly ... as they would learn in yoga. If there's good breathing in yoga, there's good breathing in karate.
Goshi Yamaguchi

I do not think the word basics is appropriate. I like to use fundamental movement, because that's what they are ... the foundation. These basics movements are extremely difficult to perform correctly.
Hajimu Takashima

If you want to be a fighter, train under a famous sensei who was a good fighter in his younger days. If you don't care about fighting and are more interested in Budo, look for a dojo with good people and a real dedicated sensei, even if he is not the greatest fighter.
Jon Bluming

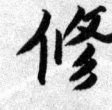

The teacher should allocate time for personal training. According to his age, he needs to develop and maintain other physical elements such as agility, limberness, endurance and good health. These elements require specific training sessions separate from karate training.
Kunio Miyake

Strengthening a part of some muscles—and not all that are used for a technique —is not harmonious. Thus, a practitioner's motion may become slow and inaccurate.
Koss Yokota

It is essential for a senior karate-ka to have a constructive, planned and monitored physical training program. As for the mind, hopefully wisdom will improve with age and influence the approach and practice of the art.
Malcolm Dorfman

Karate Wisdom

You must learn not only how to make karate natural to you but also how to strengthen your body without stressing it more than necessary.
Masahiko Tanaka

You have to be spiritually strong because karate must be spiritually strong, too. Then the correct technique will grow from it. I have seen some people who think they are strong, but the truth is they are bigheaded.
Mikio Yahara

The old masters weren't so naive when they designed the different styles. Give them the credit they deserve because there is more in the traditional styles than what meets the eye.
Ryusho Sakagami

Train hard, finish, bow and say "thank you" for the opportunity to sweat. The most important quality for a practitioner of lifetime karate is the ability to find such satisfaction in ordinary training.
Shojiro Koyama

The training under Sakagami Sensei and Mabuni Sensei was very different compared to what we see today in any martial arts school. During the war, when I began, we had no gi and no dojo. We just trained outside. We trained barefoot even when it was quite cold with snow on the ground.
Shigeru Sawabe

Training

Weightlifting creates muscle mass and a rapid increase in strength, but this kind of training works against the relaxation necessary for karate-ka to generate internal power, which is more important than muscle power.
Tetsuhiko Asai

Speed and power in karate come from correct training methods, strong conditioning and endless repetitions. I believe conditioning is one of the most important aspects of training, and I ask my students to do the same.
Teruo Chinen

When I graduated from the university, I wanted to be a professional karate teacher so I basically decided to follow Ohtsuka Sensei anywhere. I spent all my time training and teaching for Ohtsuka Sensei. The spirit was very strong and good. And the training was very hard.
Tatsuo Suzuki

Breathing is trained in goju-ryu in two important katas; sanchin and tensho. These two katas are very valuable to learn the proper way of using breathing as a tool for physical development. The breathing patterns used are ibuki, nogare and donto.
Yosuke Yamashita

The art of karate-do includes a vast spectrum of styles and each one has a special orientation and characteristic. It is not the same to train in shito-ryu as it is to train in kyokushin-kai. The important thing here is to match your needs with the right instructor and style.
Yashunari Ishimi

Karate Wisdom

The body changes and training sessions should be modified to fit these changes. Some individuals suffer injures or experience physical problems that affect what they can do and how they can do it. A person can't train the same all his life.
Yasuhiro Konishi

Repeat the basics over and over. Repetition is the key. Try to feel and develop the proper control of your muscles when performing the technique. Concentrate on correct form and the natural movement. Correct the mistakes and add speed and power little by little. Then work on timing.
Yoshiharu Osaka

In our physical movements, there are those that are natural and others that are not. Through the practice of karate-do, we can learn to differentiate between the two and also learn to acquire natural movements.
Shigeru Egami

There are many kinds of martial arts, …at a fundamental level these arts rest on the same basis. It is no exaggeration to say that the original sense of karate-do is at one with the basis of all martial arts. Form is emptiness, emptiness is form itself. The "kara" of karate-do means this.
Gichin Funakoshi

Now, karate is not for everybody—I would like to think it is, but some people are not interested in learning in depth. The right people, though, will somehow find karate.
Avi Rokah

A senior practitioner must devote time to keep his basic techniques strong and sharp but at the same time allocate time to improve and

keep moving forward. You can't always practice what you were taught 30 years ago.
Eihachi Ota

You must study your style for many, many years, and if you take from another style it must be within the laws of that particular style. The mental aspect of karate is shown in the understanding of the style, in mastering of the body itself.
Mas Oyama

Seniors need to have very clear idea of which areas they want or need to improve, and they should have specific training methods which help them achieve their goals.
Harry Cook

It is important to understand that it is sometimes necessary to return to the most basic kata to correct one specific body motion used in an advanced kata, or to perfect a point in a particular technique.
Kenzo Mabuni

In martial arts there is not a "set logic," everything is a matter of experience.
Hidetaka Nishiyama

A black belt is just the beginning of a journey. It is a degree of skill but not of ability or understanding of the teaching methods. These are two very different things.
Teruyuki Okazaki

I emphasize karate for health and tense muscles are not good for your body. But tense muscles do not come from weight training but from incorrect use of the body during training. To be able to perform good

Karate Wisdom

karate you must try to use soft and hard correctly, not always rushing and tensing your body.
Tsuguo Sakumoto

That they practice the art as a whole through kata, kumite and kihon. Today, many people train kata and kumite as if they were two different things. Actually, kumite starts with kata, and kata starts with kumite.
Takayuki Kubota

Special training is beautiful because the intense mental attitude of the students makes for a good atmosphere. Everybody tries so hard and works so hard. No one is perfect, and we all make mistakes. But no one who gets through the training has failed on any level.
Tsutomu Ohshima

When a karate-ka starts talking about hard and soft, he starts falling into dualistic thinking. The hard and the soft are not separated in true goju-ryu karate. The hard and the soft are harmoniously interwoven. It is very difficult to tell when one leaves off and the other takes over.
Anthony Mirakian

The thing that sets shotokan apart from the rest of the world is its almost pathological, philosophical and technical insistence that we always strive to create a fluid synergy between our breathing, our body actions and our techniques.
Edmond Otis

TRAINING

Oyama Sensei studied goju-ryu extensively, but one of his ideas was to start his own group, which my father approved. As a result, he started kyokushin. Even now there is still a very good friendship between the groups.
Goshi Yamaguchi

I don't think you have to go to Japan to learn how to fight like a professional, but it is real fun to go there to experience things. You can learn a lot of other things if you go and stay there for some time.
Jon Bluming

In shotokan, kime is important, but no one really taught me how to make it sharp like a whip. During my 20s and 30s, I was using too much muscle power to generate kime.
Koss Yokota

Karate training has areas in which there are physical limitations, and this is where supplementary training comes in. However, this training must be scientifically based and well monitored.
Malcolm Dorfman

If you are training in karate as a simple physical activity, you will derive less benefit as you get older.
Masahiko Tanaka

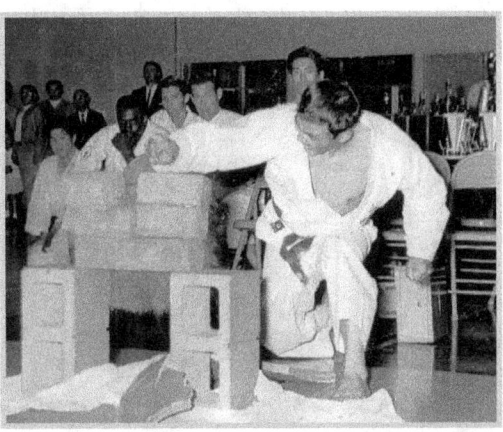

Karate Wisdom

I practice iaido. I like the spirit of this martial art. One single sword blow results in the death of the opponent.
Mikio Yahara

These martial artists who create new styles operate under the misconception that they are creating a perfect fighting method. To me, this concept is simply an illusion. The perfect style doesn't exit.
Ryusho Sakagami

If we fear aging and resent or deny the changes that accompany it, we become discontented, frustrated and ineffective in our practice of karate ... or in any other life task.
Shojiro Koyama

The main idea in fighting was not to score a point based on speed and power. Instead, it was to attack the vital points in the opponent's body. This is the reason why we develop each part of our body as a weapon.
Shigeru Sawabe

If you want to put a nail all the way into a piece of wood, you don't use a screwdriver. You use a hammer. Learn what weapons are more appropriate to hit certain parts of the human body.
Tetsuhiko Asai

As a teacher, I don't want my students to suffer the same injuries. I have done my best to develop good teaching skills that are physically harder but safer.
Teruo Chinen

Older people should not train for physical power. They have to train differently. Every action should be a softer way to bring the power from

Training

the internal organs. When they have to react to a real situation, they will be able to because of the right training.
Tatsuo Suzuki

The Ki can be used, trained and developed but your practice has to be steady and dedicated in order to open the senses for you to feel it.
Yosuke Yamashita

I have seen many practitioners run, lift weights and do other things because they think these activities will help them in karate. The truth is they don't do them to fit into the structure of the martial arts. Instead, they do them as an addition, and this prevents them from spending more time on the technical aspects that they really need to focus on to progress in their chosen art.
Yashunari Ishimi

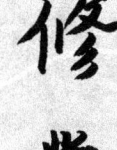

The techniques should be adapted to the age of the practitioner. A 20-year-old karate-ka is not going to do the technique the same way that a 60-year-old individual does.
Yasuhiro Konishi

Animals are not muscle bound; why should a man be? Pliancy and flexibility are natural characteristics of the human body; rigidity is the mark of death.
Shigeru Egami

Fear is a part of all human beings and exists inside us all. Training can teach a student how to deal with this fear; please note that I use the word "deal." You cannot totally eliminate the element of fear because is a feeling all human beings have.
Eihachi Ota

Karate Wisdom

Do karate to discover the mind and spirit through the body; do it to discover life through facing danger. Train to be whole.
Tatsuo Hirano

Grandmaster Higaonna, for some unknown reason, changed the name of the highest kata from the Chinese pronunciation "yepatlinpa" (meaning 108) to suparimpei.
Anthony Mirakian

Some people say you should stick with only one art ... whether that is karate or some other martial art. But my father told me that it is not good to concentrate on just one art. In the Budo, a long time ago, every samurai could study many different ways. My father felt the same way.
Goshi Yamaguchi

Subtle alterations to technique are common in all martial arts, and that has never been a problem because everyone strives for perfection. But these changes are only effective after many hours and years of research and investigation and only when the intention is to create a better and more efficient technique.
Hajimu Takashima

Without appropriate encouragement and instruction from the instructors, sho-dan students could easily get discouraged ... even to the point of giving up.
Koss Yokota

TRAINING

In the first few years of training in the JKA instructor's class in Japan, I felt fear often. I will never ever forget the feeling, day after day, as I placed my foot on the first rung of the steel spiral staircase that led to the door of the JKA Honbu dojo, wondering which instructor would smash me today.
Malcolm Dorfman

Hard, physical training helps to develop the right mind for karate. And technique isn't the only important thing; you must also make good, true karate.
Mikio Yahara

The technical foundations, which were dwelled upon for years, are unfortunately and often glossed over in a matter of a few months of part-time work. It is very important to train hard in the basics of the art.
Ryusho Sakagami

Karate Wisdom

If we think of the trophy, the tournament title or the fifth dan certificate as the ultimate "work product" of karate society, most of us will feel that, our karate seems to be purposeless.
Shojiro Koyama

Personally, I don't think that it is a good idea to study and mix styles, because it requires time and ability and a very high level of technical understanding that many people don't have.
Seinosuke Mitsuya

I don't look at karate techniques and separate the movements into advanced and basic. There are no basic or advanced movements. Techniques are the same.
Shigeru Sawabe

Flexibility is an open door for relaxation, and I make this principle my main objective. It is important to try to keep all joints loose and supple.
Tetsuhiko Asai

My need for training is spontaneous, and I will do so anytime and anywhere.
Teruo Chinen

Karate is not hard to the body if it is properly done, Unfortunately, many of the instructors around the world don't have the proper understanding to help the older students. In true karate-do, if a person is using the same kind of power when he is 60 than when he was 30, then something is wrong.
Tatsuo Suzuki

Fasting is a hygienic practice that helps you not only to keep your body clean but also to bring your chakras together in the process of developing

Training

Ki. Your hara start working in a completely different way and you are very aware of it.
Yosuke Yamashita

The teacher should teach the fundamentals of the movement and make sure students get the basic techniques down, but it is up to the students to work hard.
Yasuhiro Konishi

Sometimes even being a naturally gifted athlete can be an impediment to a practitioner's development, because those students may not have to work as hard as others in order to achieve the same level of proficiency. There is something about the discipline and determination that is forged through years of hard training, and striving to become the best you can.
Eihachi Ota

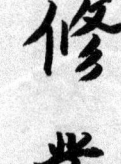

Gasshuku training is very hard and puts the practitioner in a very difficult situation, both physically and mentally.
Stan Schmidt

When Grandmaster Higaonna demonstrated his sanchin breathing kata, he would occasionally allow four Okinawans to try and dislodge him from his standing position. They could not move him. When he finished the sanchin kata, the floor where he stood would be hot from the friction of his toes gripping the floor.
Anthony Mirakian

Movements in training, when you are young, come from the muscles, tendons and ligaments. When you get old, these three elements weaken drastically and you need to have another 'source' for your physical activity. Internal training is very important, not to win tournament but for a healthy life.
H. Ohtsuka II

Karate Wisdom

Many people may think that my style of teaching is very strange, but this is only because I emphasize aspects that we usually don't see in regular karate.
Tetsuhiko Asai

We have more scientific knowledge of why and how to perform the techniques. We have become intellectually knowledgeable of the activity we practice.
Tatsuo Suzuki

In Europe, we have better teachers today than in Japan. Of course, there are few exceptions to that rule. The same goes for karate. In kendo, the Japanese are still the real masters.
Jon Bluming

The basics, which are known as kihon, apply to the art of karate-do, as well as to the foundations of Budo. It is very misleading [and wrong] if you move on and never give the basics another thought once you have learned them.
Ryusho Sakagami

Training

Forget about the secrets of the "advanced" techniques. The only "secrets" are within your body, and it is up to you to unveil these and make them work for you. Make every technique perfect.
Yasuhiro Konishi

In karate, the focus of basic training is development of the body's core, known in Japanese as the seikatanden, and its connection with the hips and legs. The triad of the seikatanden, hips and legs forms the fundamental body structure on which all stances and techniques depend.
Shojiro Koyama

Shotokan sometimes is too straight-lined. It was like a horse with blinkers on. You have to study hard, see what is missing and then try to compensate for this.
Tetsuhiko Asai

Many people regard karate training as a form of entertainment or fitness training and when it becomes too painful or demanding they move on to something else.
Harry Cook

Today, maybe the training is not as hard as it used to be, but it is more scientific. I'm not sure if this is good or bad, to be honest.
Tatsuo Suzuki

Karate Wisdom

I have found that a great many of the traditional karate teachers are now stressing bunkai training to a greater extent now than they did ten years ago. They also train the kaisetz applications of the kata, the te-gumite methods and others. But to answer your question, I am positive that without bunkai training, karate kata training becomes merely a form of ballet and the students will never truly grasp the essence of traditional karate-do.
Bill Dometrich

Kata, and its components of kihon-bunkai and oyo-bunkai, is the very essence of traditional, authentic karate. You can practice kata alone, in a small area without the need of training aids. Kata affords a serious student an opportunity to analyze—kihon-bunkai—and put to use—oyo-bunkai—the training, knowledge, and experience that the student has gained through years of training. Oyo-bunkai—to apply what you have analyzed—allows the student to develop the kata (pattern or form) and the kihon-bunkai (basic or standard analysis) on a more personal level without restrictions.
Chuck Merriman

Kata bunkai is good and necessary. Translating a kata is something very challenging. Most of the challenge is in asking yourself, "What the hell is this move for?"
Dan Ivan

Kata should not change at all. It is the traditional part of karate. Perhaps a master altered part of the kata for certain reasons, according to his practical combat experience but kata has to be kept intact in modern times. Training methods and sparring techniques may change, but not kata.
Fumio Demura

Kata

Once I began to develop some understanding of the applications of the goju kata, the shotokan kata began to make more sense, and I could see some practical or realistic ways to apply the techniques. I don't mean the silly kind of applications you usually see in demonstrations where people jump over bo attacks or perform choreographed defenses to preset karate-style attacks. I mean functional defenses to the kinds of attacks used in the street.
Harry Cook

In karate, there is the basic style or ideal, static or in coded movement as in the kata, and there is also a dynamic application in combat, where timing is of fundamental importance.
Henri Plee

The problem in the West is that many people think of themselves as masters because they know kata applications when, in fact, they can't properly perform the kata itself because they waste too much time asking instead of doing.
Morio Higaonna

Some people think that I have changed kata, but I never did. After five years of kata training, two people can practice the same movement and look identical—but after ten years differences emerge. They may think that they are doing the same movement, but since the body, character, and thoughts are different it is only natural that the kata will be different.
Hirokazu Kanazawa

For the beginners, kata is just a form, an external mold—but when you've trained for many years your understanding expands and kata becomes something else quite distinct.
Taiji Kase

Karate Wisdom

Bunkai is a very important aspect if we are interested in learning the right form of karate-do. We have to notice though, that bunkai varies depending of the style that you practice and does not always indicate the skill level of the practitioner.
Kenei Mabuni

I know some people think they don't need kata in their quest to be great fighters but they are wrong. This is an incorrect approach to karate.
Takayuki Mikami

Kata is the instrument or material used to teach students. This inheritance from the masters contains their ideology and methodology that is called the style or ryu-ha.
Minobu Miki

Kata is the symbol of karate so it never changes. Unfortunately, 95 percent of the people don't understand kata meaning—only the outside movements which are irrelevant without understanding.
Hidetaka Nishiyama

Kata requires a form which our bodies must enter. You must adapt to this because if you don't your own body will limit your style. We must train our bodies to enter into the form.
Tsuguo Sakumoto

Sensei Nishiyama rarely ever taught bunkai—in fact I can't remember when he did teach it.
Ray Dalke

KATA

Kata without bunkai is like a bite without teeth. Kata are the theorems of self-defense, whereas bunkai is the teeth and claws of karate.
Stan Schmidt

Kata can be ascribed as the interrelated fabric from which all karate is woven, understanding this formula brings an entirely new appreciation to what has long been referred to by competitors as "worthless movements," and by innovative fighters such Bruce Lee as "the classical mess."
Patrick McCarthy

The art of karate begins and finishes with kata training. There are many valuable principles and teachings within kata but there no "final answer" to every situation.
Tsuguo Sakumoto

Understanding the applications of kata is very important. Kata originated from real fighting experience, not theory. Kata is an example and a code.
Avi Rokah

Without understanding bunkai, practitioners are missing the deeper meaning behind the techniques. Many applications of the techniques found in kata are not obvious to the eye and it takes a deep study and understanding of the principles and concepts behind the movement in order to be able to find a more advanced way of using the art.
Eihachi Ota

Karate Wisdom

Although practicing a kata and improving its techniques is most important, the performance becomes incomplete and hollow without understanding and practicing its bunkai and that is exactly what is happening in competition katas.
Keiji Tomiyama

I think bunkai is very important. It brings karate to another level. When you understand bunkai a lot of things are revealed to you.
Kiyoshi Yamazaki

The martial applications themselves are swift, subtle and very lethal. They are fully effective but cannot be learned or used effectively until a considerable groundwork of exercises and form have been laid down.
Yoshinao Nanbu

The analysis of the different karate techniques found in kata is very important. You need to understand that bunkai is structured in different levels of application, with varying difficulty.
Yuishi Negishi

The kata martial applications themselves are swift, subtle and very lethal. They are fully effective but cannot be learned or used effectively until a considerable groundwork of exercises and forms has been covered.
Seiji Mishimura

It seems to me that what has happened recently is that bunkai has become a faddish way of re-arranging karate training to make it more appealing as a self-defense system.
Randall Hassell

Kata

Bunkai helps the student understand the kata. It teaches us timing, balance, and reaction. It is unfortunate that the modern karate is moving away from bunkai.
Val Mijailovic

Bunkai is a person's interpretation of what a movement means, and this interpretation differs from person to person. I believe that everyone should break down a kata and see how many scenarios you can come up with. It's called "thinking for yourself."
Wally Slocki

Self-defense karate has to be trained for specifically, and kata bunkai is the main tool for this.
Gogen Yamaguchi

I appreciate the overall understanding that learning kata from another style brings to a karate practitioner. It opens a lot of possibilities and helps you to look at your own style in a different way.
Alex Sternberg

The word "kata" also means "symbol." The kata symbolizes certain principles of movement and combat that the kata originators wanted to transmit to us.
Avi Rokah

They say kata is fighting against an imaginary opponent. Well, when I want to fight, I fight against a live opponent. That's why I don't believe in kata.
Dominique Valera

Karate Wisdom

In kata, there are no surprises—the movements and sequences are the same all the time. The important aspect is that the practitioner develop what we call "internal timing." This means to coordinate the joints and hips with the delivery of the techniques.
Eihachi Ota

The importance attached to kata makes it one of the most recognizable features in all of martial arts. Kata was the creation of the most important teachers of each style of karate in the past.
Keinosuke Enoeda

The more I study kata, the more I can see how important they are for fighting. To fight better than your opponent, you must make him move as you want—with proper spirit, and well-balanced techniques. Your technique has power when your body moves as a single unit. Kata helps you learn that unity.
Katsutaka Tanaka

I think that sparring should be taught first in karate. After you've learned how to move that way you should progress on to learning kata. If you look at the really good kata competitors you can see they have an understanding of kumite. Their kata is real and alive.
Yukiyoshi Marutani

Kata in an integral part of the art of karate. In fact, karate can't be totally understood without a thorough study of kata.
Yuishi Negishi

KATA

A kata is a work of art, just like a painting by an old master. When you look at the painting you try to see it in the light that the artist painted it. You study it and find the meaning the artist was trying to convey through the medium of oil and canvas.
Seiji Mishimura

Kata teaches fighting skills and living skills at the same time. The aim of kata is to make the individual one with the universe, attuned to the kata.
Richard Kim

Real attacks are thwarted by mastery of the core principles of awareness, timing, distancing, conditioned reflexes, strong technique, and stable emotions under attack, among other things. Kata training is excellent for developing these things.
Randall Hassell

If you look closely you'll see that in the very end all the "secret" kata are no more than bad versions of authentic forms. It's sad, but many of these false masters are getting away with telling their fairy tales.
Shinpo Matayoshi

We do a lot of kata and they have all the self-defense techniques, takedowns, and choking techniques. I believe you just strike a balance.
Shigeru Oyama

In the kata aspect, just because a Westerner wins a world title it doesn't mean they are better than a Japanese or Okinawan performing kata. Kata has nothing to do with the acrobatic performances that we see today.
Tamas Weber

Karate Wisdom

Kata gives us the means of remembering and paying tribute to our teachers. It gives us the tool for testing ourselves. Kata tunes and refines our energy flow and it allows us to unite energetically and spiritually.
Val Mijailovic

Kata training can be divided in two simple aspects—the actual performance of the form and the application and use of the techniques found in the form. If you are good at performing the kata but you don't have a deep understanding of how to use the techniques of the form, then your training is meaningless.
Gogen Yamaguchi

Otsuka sensei was always looking for "quality" and not "quantity" in everything he did. This approach conditioned his point of view and therefore his mentality in karate-do. He never looked for a lot of kata because you can't really master 50 or 60 kata.
Yoshiaki Ajari

If one removes the bunkai from kata, it becomes a superficial practice in which meaningless maneuvers simply become a dance and nothing more. The "guts" of kata lie in its bunkai or what can be practiced as kyogi-kumite.
Tino Ceberano

Bunkai is essential to karate. This tendency to move away from bunkai represents separating sport karate from the whole traditional system.
Tatsuo Hirano

The idea, as Funakoshi Sensei showed in the later years of his life, is that it is nonsense to memorize dozens of kata. It is ridiculous.
Tsutomu Ohshima

KATA

There can be no such thing as a perfect kata and we can go deeper and deeper into one kata and continue to uncover hidden skill. This process too is never ending.
Akio Minakami

My personal philosophy and, to a great extent, the official stated philosophy of the AJKA, is that bunkai really is not the main reason that we practice kata.
Edmond Otis

Kata is of the utmost importance. Kata is like the culture for the school. Goju has goju ideas, and these are in the kata. That is why we must study one standard.
Goshi Yamaguchi

I have been hearing all my life criticisms about how useless kata training is for real self-defense but I haven't heard more than few people talking about the distinction between the concept of any particular kata and the physical form.
H. Ohtsuka II

Kihon is nothing more than movements from kata practiced individually. The techniques from kata were extracted and put in a kihon format in order to perfect them individually. If you understand this point, it will change the way you look at the connection between kihon, kata and kumite.
Hajimu Takashima

In order to do a kata well, you have to "mold" your body so it "shows" the karate movement with precision and proper technique.
Kunio Miyake

Karate Wisdom

If you do a kata without thinking, that kata will be not too far off from a dance. If a movement or an application does not make sense in a kata, the student must challenge the movement and investigate it until it does.
Koss Yokota

To perform a kata with feeling and passion, one must be able to visualize an opponent or opponents. This is not possible without understanding the bunkai of that particular kata.
Malcolm Dorfman

When you see a kata performed well, you realize that immediately. As artists, we all strive for perfection. In our case, we should strive for perfection in technique, even though we will never achieve it.
Masahiko Tanaka

Forms are composed of single movements or parts that make up the whole form. To become an expert, you should strive to learn how to use these parts.
Ryusho Sakagami

Like most things, bunkai training has both advantages and disadvantages. On the negative side, for any technique, there may be another more reasonable or more efficient application or countermove than what is typically taught in bunkai training. On the other hand, if one is interested in brain stimulation, training and the right hemisphere in particular, bunkai training can be very helpful because it helps develop imagination and spatial perception.
Shojiro Koyama

Kata is essential to karate. Kata organizes the technical foundation of the style from the base (kihon) to very high levels of technical expertise.
Seinosuke Mitsuya

We didn't really care at all about the look of our kata. This is something that you see today. At that time, kata was not for show. By this, I mean that we never tried to make it look good. It was like a textbook in which you could take technical information.
Shigeru Sawabe

The essence of the form is still there and nothing has changed, but the personal flavor the instructor put into it [changed] because of his evolution as a martial artist.
Tetsuhiko Asai

Kata must stay the same, but the concept of the form must change in relation to the culture of the country where the instructor is teaching.
Teruo Chinen

Today there are many differences in kata, and I honestly think that they are irrelevant because they display only the personal flavor incorporated by the teacher. A lot of the time the arguments are simply nonsense.
Yashunari Ishimi

My father developed the kata seiryu in collaboration with Mabuni Sensei. Kenwa Mabuni's influence in Shindo Jinen Ryu is evident in the kata syllabus of ryobu-kai.
Yasuhiro Konishi

Karate Wisdom

The final point of the movement is not as important as the transitional phases between them. The only way to correct this is focusing is in strong kihon practice.
Yoshiharu Osaka

Kata teaches you the movements and body mechanics; kumite allows you to practice those movements with a partner, either in a pre-arranged way or in a free situation. This essentially is what bunkai is.
Harry Cook

I'm against changing kata. I believe that kata is not just something that someone made up. They are hundreds and thousands of years old. There is a lot of information in each one of them.
Morio Higaonna

The classical or the traditional movement found in kata is one thing and the way you directly apply them in a real situation is another. The body mechanics may be the same but the flavor of the combat application is different because your state of mind is different.
Kenei Mabuni

The analysis of one single kata may take years; by this I mean the different uses of the same technique, and its application in kumite and self-defense. I recommend to study deeply one or two kata.
Takayuki Mikami

Kata cannot be just remembered in the mind only. Many physical repetitions are necessary to add it to the memory as well as perfecting each movement within the form.
Minobu Miki

Kata

The student must copy the designs for a long time and, in the end, once he has picked up the principles, develop his own way.
Hidetaka Nishiyama

Sensei Funakoshi took me with him to visit Sensei Mabuni and he told me to learn two kata from him—ninjushijo and gojushijo—so we could study them later on in detail and more carefully.
Masatoshi Nakayama

I think that kata is a wonderful way to develop the practitioner. Every kata has its strong points and if one doesn't have a way of working the triceps or hamstring we have another kata that does work those areas.
Ray Dalke

Kata must be memorized, incorporated into one's own being and then mastered to perfection. It is essential to break into areas of techniques that are original. Kata training offers a way of understand other aspects of human existence, that's why is so important not to study the form from a strictly structural point of view.
Keinosuke Enoeda

Kata are the time capsules of karate whose techniques, when properly understood, reveal practical responses to the habitual acts of physical violence which plagued early Chinese society.
Patrick McCarthy

Kata only teaches three corners of the room. When the original masters structured kata, they were trying to teach something. It's up to the student to find the fourth corner. Using kata, we can train and teach karate until the last days of life.
Tsuguo Sakumoto

Karate Wisdom

I worry that some will emphasize this bunkai training over actual practice of the kata itself, and I think that's bad. A balance between the two is very important.
Randall Hassell

The techniques the old master incorporated into the katas, and their technical solution to the problems, were based on the circumstances, environment and technologies of that particular time.
Wally Slocki

Kata is a composition of basic movements. The purpose of kata is to teach the body to move in a variety of ways, using different type of techniques. Once you understand that, you'll see that kumite is just having the ability to move your body freely like in kata—but this time against an opponent.
Alex Sternberg

Of course, kata is limited—it is a form. We cannot apply kata in a real fight. Principles, on the other hand, are not limited. They are formless and they can be adapted to any circumstances. When we internalize the principles of kata, we can apply karate techniques to any self-defense circumstances.
Avi Rokah

When studying kata, we can see a model for a particular method of certain techniques. There is a formalized way of doing things but kata also offers freedom of expression. Not only the techniques of the creator, but also the acquisition of the right state of mind called "kokoro."
Keinosuke Enoeda

The more time you spend exploring a kata, the deeper will be your understanding of the art of karate and its uses. You have to go deeper and deeper into the study of the kata. You just can't stop on the surface and simply try to master the physical and external appearance of the kata.
Katsutaka Tanaka

Kata is simply a moving work of art. It was a means of communication for artists who lived thousand of years ago. The message is there and is very clear. You don't have to intellectualize it or sit in front of it and mediate. All you have to do is perform the movements in order to understand the message.
Seiji Mishimura

Sparring and self-defense with partners are part of the instruction, but it is kata training that is most important. Kata is the primary path to self-mastery of the individual.
Richard Kim

Karate Wisdom

Changing the technique to make it more appealing to the judges and increasing the breathing volume to pretend to have more kime is a joke to the real art of karate-do.
Tamas Weber

In the early days, we practiced a lot of basics and kata. Kata was broken down into segments that we trained repetitively. Nowadays the emphasis is on the overall physical performance of the form, not in the self-defense principles hidden in the kata and their combative value as fighting tools.
Gogen Yamaguchi

All traditional katas are greatly respected in the martial arts, and you can search your entire life to find the deeper meanings of a particular form. Moreover, the beauty of refinement (kohga) and the elegant simplicity (sabi) are also important kata training elements.
Keinosuke Enoeda

Mabuni sensei became a living encyclopedia of kata but he was a real exception in Budo history. He was a very talented and dedicated man. Unfortunately, today we don't have the time to train 60 kata every single day.
Yoshiaki Ajari

Kata contains waza and its teachings of waza are done with bunkai training. You can take each kata application segment and turn it into a waza drill for kumite.
Tatsuo Hirano

In the Western world, the people think that if you know 60 kata, you are better than the practitioner who knows only 30. And that is wrong. This exemplifies a process of accumulation in which the truth is that true Budo and true karate are just the opposite. It is about simplification.
Tsutomu Ohshima

KATA

This is the true wisdom left for us in kata by the ancient Ryukyu warriors. It is up to us to discover, temper and polish this wisdom.
Akio Minakami

Trying to make the kata movement (mold) fit into a real self-defense situation doesn't work most of the time, because, unfortunately, the instructors and associations around the world have been more interested in making the kata look good than in doing the techniques as they should be done in a real situation.
Hajimu Takashima

Ultimately, the goal of karate training is a marriage of physical mastery, emotional stability and intellectual focus. Kata develops all three of those in a synchronized and congruent fashion.
Edmond Otis

Kata is about the battle within yourself.
Goshi Yamaguchi

Kata helps karate-ka to understand the many uses the techniques and how to apply them. Without kata training, one is not following the way of martial arts. Profound technique is one of the main benefits of kata training.
Keinosuke Enoeda

The fighting concept behind any kata is completely valid for self-protection but very few people understand this. Every single kata, regardless of the style, has a concept and principle behind it. It is this what is relevant. It is here where lies the true meaning of kata training.
H.Ohtsuka II

Karate Wisdom

The applications bunkai and onyo-bunkai that I teach are the result of my instructors' influence and of my own experience and understanding of how the basic principles of a particular technique may be used in a real situation.
Hajimu Takashima

Depending on the style, kata has different sets of the principles that help you to develop the "flavor" in the art of karate.
Kunio Miyake

Kata teaches you the sequences of attacking and defending moves or combinations, body shifting and turning, and some non-standard techniques that you generally do not practice often in kihon.
Koss Yokota

Kata, performed with grace and Ki, can ignite the imagination, inspire the spirit and provide meaning to one's practice of karate, as well as foster an appreciation for solid fundamental techniques.
Shojiro Koyama

I think that the best way to learn is to have a good and competent master who can truly teach you the essence of the form, its meaning and its applications, many of which are hidden, both for self-defense and for the health of the person.
Seinosuke Mitsuya

I understand that modern practitioners do not need to study 60 or 70 kata, but Mabuni Sensei was in a very important position in the history

KATA

of Budo. He was the link between several styles in Okinawa and the acceptance of karate in Japan.
Shigeru Sawabe

Kata represents the history of the art. All the tradition in these forms [has been] passed down from masters to students throughout the generations.
Tetsuhiko Asai

Sanchin teaches the student how to properly use oxygen and send it to all the parts of the body. This kata also helps to judge the student's level when practicing other forms. I do believe that strong basics are the secrets to becoming a good karate-ka.
Teruo Chinen

In kata you can personalize the movement, but you have to be aware of the essential meaning and principle behind the technique. And this shouldn't be altered at all.
Yashunari Ishimi

After many months of research and training, my father developed a kata called "Tai Sabaki." He based this kata on karate, but he incorporated principles found in the teachings of Ueshiba Sensei. Though the new kata did not contain any complex movements, it consisted of a chain of actions

Karate Wisdom

with no pause after each action. After Konishi Sensei demonstrated this kata, Ueshiba Sensei remarked that, "The demonstration you did just now was satisfactory to me, and that kata is worth mastering."
Yasuhiro Konishi

Kata should be kept as the original form that was developed. Kata represent the history of our art, and we can't change it as we please.
Yoshiharu Osaka

If you are interested in the more traditional approach then first learn the kata and then practice all the different ways you can apply the techniques. For seniors, simply going through the movements of the kata in thin air, polishing the outer form of the techniques, might have some kind of aerobic value; but I feel it is more productive to actually practice the applications of the techniques in a variety of situations.
Harry Cook

The kata keeps the meaning of the technique deep. It makes one fresh to respond. Knowledge of the art increases because self-defense is found in kata. Without kata training, the body cannot properly understand the technique.
Keinosuke Enoeda

Kata must be done as if your opponent were real. In kata you do not memorize your movements, but the imaginary opponent's attack. You can always do beautiful kata, but if you don't put concentration into it, kata will be dead. Kata must be alive.
Seiji Mishimura

Knowing the bunkai is not enough. If the movement is not mature then the Art will be low level.
Akio Minakami

Kata

Traditional kata are like "technique reservoirs" where some additional movements were added by the old master only to be able of practicing them in a sequential order.
H. Ohtsuka II

Kata should stay traditional, as it was passed down by the old masters. I don't like to see kata transformed using the gymnastics approach because it looks better for competition.
Hajimu Takashima

Kata should not be practiced without kumite in mind. Kata without knowing the meaning of each movement might be a dance.
Koss Yokota

Never forsake one kata for another and treat them all the same because they bring different benefits to you. Dedicate yourself to your instructor. When you become a teacher, teach anyone who is willing to learn.
Shigeru Sawabe

The kata were structured and formatted by the old masters to preserve realistic knowledge of self-defense. It is very important to study the form and to understand what you are doing and why are you doing it.
Tetsuhiko Asai

What we need to keep constant is the principle of the kata and not necessarily the specific details of the minor technical movements.
Yashunari Ishimi

The real challenge is in every time we do the movement and in every single time we repeat the kata. There is no goal in kata training. The goal is the training itself.
Yoshiharu Osaka

Karate Wisdom

Bunkai has its place in kata, and kata has its place in the art of karate-do. It is important to be knowledgeable about the bunkai of every kata but we have to be careful. Why do you think modern anti-terrorist groups change their approach to an emergency situation and security systems are evolving all the time? Because the terrorists are using new methods more advanced that those used 20 years ago. The same happens with kata, bunkai, and martial arts in general.
Wally Slocki

Kata training is very necessary for taking part in sport karate. This keeps techniques fresh and it is also important because it develops the body properly. It is necessary to keep fit for the art.
Keinosuke Enoeda

Kata is a repository of knowledge passed down throughout generations, and the information contained is extremely valuable. If we take kata only as a training method and not as a well of information for self-defense, then the bunkai and onyo bunkai don't exist.
Hajimu Takashima

Simply because you don't understand a kata doesn't mean there is something wrong with it. If you change a kata before your understanding reaches the level the kata is on, you'll be defeating the purpose of the kata.
Seiji Mishimura

We have to simplify, simplify and simplify what we do. Quality in our acts, not quantity. Quality in our kata, not quantity of forms.

KATA

If you know 20 kata, then make 10 better. If you only know 10, make five extremely good.
Tsutomu Ohshima

Kata teaches us to develop intense moment-by-moment focus, while at the same time, maintaining an overall awareness of ourselves in relation to the world around us ... the whole.
Edmond Otis

It is important to understand kata for what it is and evaluate its relevancy as a great traditional training method that supplies a lot of efficient information for all karate-ka.
H. Ohtsuka II

Don't change kata for the appearance. If you have to change or modify something in the form, do it for its efficiency and effectiveness in application. Do it for a practical reason.
Hajimu Takashima

In kata, each style has its own character and flavor that shows the roots of the style. Therefore, mixing styles creates difficulty with mastering a true technique.
Kunio Miyake

Kata without studying bunkai or knowing the meaning of a movement is nearly a dance. Although bunkai is important, there is a pitfall with

KARATE WISDOM

it. As some of the instructors either do not understand the meaning of the movements or try to be creative, they come up with strange and unrealistic applications to the movements.
Koss Yokota

Each kata represents and teaches certain fighting principles.
Shigeru Sawabe

I encourage each student to examine all of the movements in all kata and try to understand the applications and true meanings.
Koss Yokota

The variations in the use and study of the forms bring new perspectives and ideas to the kata, and this is always good for the art. The main idea is to use the kata as a training method and the bunkai as the actual application in combat.
Tetsuhiko Asai

In Okinawa, tensho kata is considered to be at the same level as pechurin [suparimpei], but I always teach it to beginners so they can develop the proper breathing pattern and greater lung capacity.
Teruo Chinen

The art of karate and kata—as part of it—shouldn't be altered to the point that the essence of what the art is all about gets lost.
Yashunari Ishimi

The fact that different kata origins influenced the principles and concepts behind the forms. If a shotokan instructor thinks that it can be beneficial to incorporate a shito-ryu or goju-ryu kata into the curriculum to fill some gaps of the shotokan style, there is nothing wrong with that.
Yasuhiro Konishi

KATA

In order to understand kata, it is important that the practitioners understand the process and evolution of that particular form.
Yoshiharu Osaka

When you perform your kata alone, your knowledge of the applications brings the kata to life; without this interplay between kata and kumite the kata have no meaning except as exercise.
Harry Cook

I always say that kata is like a printed letter. The are portraits of the basic techniques and history. If you change the essence of kata, you loose all this.
Morio Higaonna

Your preferences in kata change with your age and evolution. Some kata may be very difficult for me but easy for you and vice versa. It is the person's ability that causes the difficulty.
Taiji Kase

Curiously enough, bunkai doesn't make you a good karate-ka—kihon, kata practice, and kumite do. Don't be mistaken.
Kenei Mabuni

Kata teaches the correct body positioning, the proper execution of the techniques, focus, balance, et cetera. One gains powerful techniques from correctly using the body. Why do you think the best kata people are the best fighters?
Takayuki Mikami

I do not have a favorite kata, but I have learned a few kata directly from the heir of shito-ryu, Soke Kenzo Mabuni, which were left unpublished by his father and founder, Kenwa Mabuni.
Minobu Miki

Karate Wisdom

Kata is karate. All karate techniques are taken from kata. Original kata is very valuable.
Hidetaka Nishiyama

Kata is like a song in a foreign language—unless you understand the language the song is sung in, its meaning will forever remain a mystery.
Patrick McCarthy

Kata is the essence of karate but it depends a lot on the individual. The performer's spirit brings every kata to life. An understanding of what you are doing makes the difference.
Tsugo Sakumoto

Kata teaches how each technique is to be performed in terms of body movements. It conditions the body and the mind. With kata training you reach a higher level of fitness. All you techniques are sharp and fresh.
Keinosuke Enoeda

KATA

Kata is very important because it makes you develop awareness.
Seiji Mishimura

When looking at bunkai, we need to study the principles and try to apply them in a realistic environment. Self-defense does not always have to do with physical techniques.
Yoshiharu Osaka

Kata training is of foremost importance, and adherence to the original form a must. The masters who created the kata movements did so in a state of enlightenment, and it should be the student's goal to practice repeatedly in an attempt to attain that same state of awareness.
Richard Kim

Kata is not simply the memorization of a series of movements. I'm a very creative person. I could have created 100 new kata, but what and why? Kata training is the opposite of that. Kata is for the spirit, for your own maturity.
Tsutomu Ohshima

There is no limit to the secrets hidden in the kata. I am not talking about bunkai. I am talking about natural movement: how to take one step forward or make one turn. Often, this requires a very sophisticated level of kihon or basics.
Akio Minakami

Karate Wisdom

Kata is an accumulation of the excellent moves that were used by the experts of the past and it is a textbook of fighting movements.
Koss Yokota

Don't try to make sense of the complete kata at once because it was never meant to be that way. Pay attention to the little details in the structure of the form. There is more than meets the eye.
Shigeru Sawabe

You can also use different kata to develop different attributes and qualities. Not all kata are designed for the same thing.
Tetsuhiko Asai

Miyagi Sensei broke the different kata into a wide variety of applied physical situations that could be used in self-defense scenarios.
Teruo Chinen

You have to focus on keeping the real essence of the form with the proper global rhythm and pace. That's what you should keep in mind. If you do that, then a little modification on the speed of a hand movement or sequence won't matter at all.
Yashunari Ishimi

Knowing all shotokan kata without having the proper understanding and feeling for each form is useless. Personal expression of the art must be emphasized here.
Yoshiharu Osaka

In kata there is only space and time and you. There is no opponent—nothing to grasp—you have to imagine and aim for a spiritual opponent.
Morio Higaonna

Your mind has to be in control before, during and after the execution of the form. This is a very difficult part of karate training where kata becomes a kind of meditation. Reaching this level is extremely difficult and only then can you say "the kata is mine." Your mind takes control over everything else.
Kenei Mabuni

Many unpublished kata that Kenwa Mabuni left behind are very interesting. I am proud to be one of the only people in the world who knows these kata.
Minobu Miki

The practitioner must first study the kata at the outside form, but seek the principles. Kata is like saying "for example." You must study and understand—not just look at the outside form which is just an example.
Hidetaka Nishiyama

My personal feeling is that the karate professional must spend three years on a kata and three months in kumite as a proper ratio.
Kenzo Mabuni

Kata is the instructional material or textbook of each style and thus is essential to that style. Many traditional instructors do not know the correct bunkai or oyo, much less the meaning and purpose of kakushi-waza or the hidden techniques.
Minobu Miki

Some people have very strong kata but are not beautiful. This is because they have not made the kata match their body.
Hidetaka Nishiyama

Karate Wisdom

Learning kata without its corresponding philosophy creates a terrible imbalance, which is usually reflected in attitude, character, and behavior. Understanding kata is simply a matter of understanding facts.
Patrick McCarthy

Long ago, kata was practiced as a series of self-defense situations against an imaginary opponent, but if you interpret kata like that nowadays, I think your progress will stop there. You must try to find a balance between these two different aspects.
Seiji Mishimura

Different styles have different references, so if the bunkai of a style is not practiced properly, then there can be no true understanding of what the movements represent.
Kunio Miyake

Nowadays, I see students all over the world trying to collect as many katas as they can from different styles, rather than spend time and energy internalizing the information. With that kata collector mentality, the practitioner won't go very far in their karate training. Knowledge is very important but

going around accumulating forms and kata is not the best idea. It means nothing in the true way of karate-do.
Yoshiaki Ajari

The idea is to become one with what you do, with the kata, with the physical movement. You express your best with all of your energy. That is the direction of the true karate. And kata training is for that. To invent a new kata to impress a bunch of people is not karate ... it is being a Hollywood star.
Tsutomu Ohshima

If you take a kata and train it in its whole dimension you'll find out that it takes years to master the 'mold' of basic format. Then, you have to go into the bunkai of it. And master it, which it takes more years. Later you have to go deeper into the hidden aspects of each movement and onyo-bunkai, which is not so obvious and easy. Only then you can put all the aspects of the form and study the concept behind it and how it applies to fighting and life itself. This process takes many years for a single kata, so how are you going to go deep into 40 different kata in a lifetime?
H.Ohtsuka II

We must take kata and practice all the movements in a precise way because these actions must be interpreted in a practical manner and become kumite.
Hajimu Takashima

Kata is the central element in the three aspects of karate. Without it, we can't have kihon and kumite.
Hajimu Takashima

Karate Wisdom

Study the bunkai and oyo-bunkai, research the history of kata and find the true meaning behind the form. To be a master of shito-ryu doesn't necessarily mean you need to know 60 different kata.
Shigeru Sawabe

You need to know what your weak points are and choose the kata that will help you to improve those. That's when kata becomes a training method for specific purposes.
Tetsuhiko Asai

Sometimes you find that the bunkai is applied in a different direction or using other principles to make it effective in combat. If you don't know how to unlock these principles and techniques, you may never find the real reason behind the technique.
Teruo Chinen

You can practice a traditional kata and perform it beautifully in a tournament without having to alter and modify the original form to look better in front of the judges.
Yashunari Ishimi

Nakayama Sensei used kata as a training method for achieving technical perfection and bringing all the necessary attributes to the body of the practitioner.
Yoshiharu Osaka

Kata is not just a bunch of basic techniques organized in sequences. Kata is for the integration of the practitioner's mind and imagination.
Kenzo Mabuni

KATA

The practice of bunkai should be carried out slowly for a better understanding—at least at first. Once the bunkai is understood, then it must be practiced at full speed. Otherwise, there is no reason for doing bunkai—it's pointless. Kata without the element of realism is a waste of time.
Minobu Miki

The old masters would first study the outside actions of the kata then digest it. They would make the kata their own, but not by changing the techniques and movements, but making it match their own body.
Hidetaka Nishiyama

Historically, kata has always been the principal vehicle through which the art of karate has been taught. It was Bruce Lee who, in an effort to promote his eclectic training concepts, referred to ritualized practices such as kata, as the "classical mess."
Patrick McCarthy

Each kata has its specification, and it has to be used for that specific purpose. This is one of the reasons why it seems that Mabuni Sensei used the naha-te forms in the beginning of the student's training. Maybe he used that to develop the body so he could later introduce more subtle technical actions based on speed [shuri-te].
Shigeru Sawabe

I know about 140 different forms from different styles of martial arts, and each and every one of them teaches me something different, but I am Japanese and my karate is Japanese. A shotokan practitioner shouldn't be fixated on only training the 26 standard kata of the style.
Tetsuhiko Asai

Karate Wisdom

If kata movement goes to the right, you must think the answer is to the left. If one looks at the sky, then the enemy may be on the ground. Leave 10 percent of your karate a mystery and enjoy it. Use your imagination.
Teruo Chinen

Having five cars in your garage does not make you a better driver. Kata training is not about quantity ... it is about quality.
Yashunari Ishimi

Karate self-defense lies in kata bunkai.
Yasuhiro Konishi

Technical precision is critical. Focus on the intention of the movement and learn the proper timing, tempo and rhythm of the form. Keep maximum concentration while training and the correct attitude throughout the kata.
Yoshiharu Osaka

Kata teaches you some intricate moves and sequences that you normally would not practice in basics.
Koss Yokota

The demands of kata competition have caused kata to evolve in ways opposed to the traditional criteria. In these contests, kata is purely performed for the visual effect of the movements.
Kenzo Mabuni

I visited Master Kenwa Mabuni's shito ryu dojo to learn kata from him. His kata was very beautiful. He had a very skillful body.
Hidetaka Nishiyama

Make no mistake about it, however, if kata was meant for actually combating warriors of the battlefield or confronting prizefighters in an arena, its training methods would be diametrically opposite to what has been classically handed down.
Patrick McCarthy

The heritage we have received from the old masters represents a thousand years of experience and knowledge. Kata is karate's history, and you don't re-write history.
Hajimu Takashima

The student has to go deeper into the meaning and application of every single movement and principle found in the forms. And this is a lifetime study because many of the real techniques are hidden in onyo-bunkai.
Yashunari Ishimi

A wise teacher will remind students not to place too much weight on how they compare with others in the dojo.
Masahiro Okada

Kumite

組手

Karate Wisdom

My technique is dependent on skill not mere strength. Now in sparring I don't fight my opponent—I get in tune with him, set him up, and then use his technique to my advantage.
Avi Rokah

I didn't like the idea of being that close to my opponent. I didn't enjoy fighting at close range. I prefer to have greater distance between my opponent and myself.
Dominique Valera

Kumite develops what we call "external timing." The practitioner must adjust to changing circumstances and learn to master distance and space. The bottom line is that both are critical for success in a self-defense situation.
Eihachi Ota

Sport sparring is not self-defense and has very little to do with it. Sparring is a test of ability, but ability of a different kind.
Keinosuke Enoeda

For four years I did professional kickboxing. The reason is because I wanted to work on some different things. I also wanted to see if my karate would work, so to speak. Although the techniques are different, there are some common threads that you can use in order to make karate more real and contact oriented.
Hideharu Igaki

It's a rather simple concept, but it's very difficult to teach. What it boils down to is a person's ability to refuse to be beaten. Injury and pain must be accepted as minor obstacles. The ultimate concern is to prevail and to convince yourself that nothing else matters.
Katsutaka Tanaka

Kumite

Kumite in the dojo or in competition and street fighting are two different ways of fighting. Training in kumite will help keep you in shape for any type of fighting; however, actual kumite techniques are not a part of street fighting.
Kiyoshi Yamazaki

The defect of karate fighters is that they don't know how to use a good right hand like a boxer does. The good boxer will only use the right hand once he has feinted. It's important to understand this to fully apply a karate blow.
Richard Kim

There are many styles of karate that do not engage in free-fighting, and they have produced a number of people that I would consider to be very formidable fighting machines in the street.
Randall Hassell

Knowledge is power. A real fighting art should be based on principles that allow you to use and interrelate all your techniques against any type of attack.
Shinpo Matayoshi

The 100 man kumite is the hardest thing I ever did in my life! You don't fight one-hundred men with your body—it's your spirit that keeps you going.
Shigeru Oyama

The martial artist, before a fight begins, should feel like a warrior in the battlefield and have a short moment of stress mixed with fear. Then when you control your fear and stress, you turn it into a source of a positive energy and use it as a power source to neutralize and destroy the challenger or the target.
Tamas Weber

KARATE WISDOM

The art of karate is a self-defense method. All I can say is that karate-do is a martial art and as such it is as effective as any other martial arts style—but the important point here is the level and skill of the practitioner.
Gogen Yamaguchi

If you have to think you've been already hit. I used drills to develop stamina, awareness, and kime. Later on, you put all the elements together to make them work in kumite. On a mental level, I always stressed that every fighter should find their exclusive routine or ritual in order to build up their energy and spirit.
Chuck Merriman

Free-fighting is really important, whether you do it with equipment or without. It gives you speed, timing, and distancing that you can use if someone attacks you. Good free-fighters can simply outmaneuver the average person that comes swinging and kicking wildly.
Dan Ivan

When I entered my first competition, for example, I managed to knock out my opponent with a back elbow to the solar plexus. I was really proud and I couldn't understand why I was disqualified. No one had ever told me to pull or mute the strikes in sparring.
Harry Cook

In Okinawa, the art is practiced as a method of self-exploration, as an internal research, without focusing on fighting. And this is perfect for those who look for that particular goal but for those who look at karate as a fighting art, competition is necessary.
Teruo Hayashi

Karate without test is not real karate. One great Japanese expert said, "What use is a magnificent, well balanced sword if one is incapable of using it? Better to posses a wooden sword and be skilful with it."
Henri Plee

Kumite is handwriting, and everybody has their own penmanship! In sparring, you have an opponent and it's a little bit easier because you adapt to the movements of your adversary.
Morio Higaonna

The basic idea is to establish harmony within yourself—harmonize your breathing, your movements, and your power. This will lead you to harmonize with the opponent.
Hirokazu Kanazawa

Real karate is not just jumping around and grazing your opponent. It's concentration and bang! Game over. You have to think about a life-or-death situation. Karate is a martial art which is practiced bare-handed.
Taiji Kase

KARATE WISDOM

Kumite is a misunderstood aspect these days. Kumite is not sport competition. Sport is one aspect of kumite.
Kenei Mabuni

Kumite is the application of the techniques—kumite for fun, kata for learning.
Minobu Miki

Without practice against an opponent, we cannot have the chance to work at our greatest capacity. Fighting is dangerous, but fighting is indispensable. Only through it can we maintain the essential skills of karate.
Masatoshi Nakayama

The more free-fighting one does with different opponents, especially at a young age, the better. It is imperative to improving one's judgement and effectiveness and will condition you against someone trying to rob or injure you.
Stan Schmidt

You need different techniques because people are different—and you need to have tools to deal with different kinds of opponents. This is the reason why it is so important to spar against many different stylists.
Takayuki Kubota

The best way to improve your skills and understanding of the mind in responsive action is to spar.
Tino Ceberano

You should first penetrate your opponent with your mind and technique will follow.
Tsutomu Ohshima

KUMITE

In a real self-defense situation, the attacker is not looking for a sparring partner to test his skills but for a victim.
H. Ohtsuka II

Otsuka Sensei realized the limitation of some traditional blocking techniques in actual combat and began to modify the technical structure of the techniques to better fit into a realistic fighting situation.
Hajimu Takashima

I never agreed with the so-called old system in which you are not allowed to touch or hit your opponent.
Jon Bluming

Unfortunately, modern kumite does not show the characteristics of each ryu anymore because everything is extremely unified in movement and approach. This is the result of sport competition.
Kunio Miyake

In kumite, most of the time, you do not dictate the time. You need to think of the distance, timing and target, in addition to the stances and the very technique to apply. But, of course, you only have a few seconds—or less—to decide. So, it becomes more important to think through the technique and other factors both before and after the kumite exercise.
Koss Yokota

I appreciate the toughness of kickboxing and the hard training that is necessary, but I fail to understand why people want to deliberately knock each other out. On the other hand, to know you have the power, both mentally and physically—without having to implement it

Karate Wisdom

unnecessarily to the detriment of another human being—is an objective and art worthy of a lifelong study and practice.
Malcolm Dorfman

I love to fight and that urge was with me for some time. Now that I have it out of my system, I don't get upset about the outcome of a fight. The ultimate aim of karate lies not in victory or defeat.
Masahiko Tanaka

The instructors taught us to punch and kick to defeat the opponent so our mentality was simply to attack. Of course, when we got seriously hit, we had to figure out how to block!
Tatsuo Suzuki

We used kicks to the legs, headbutts, attacks to the groin, et cetera. It was—without a doubt—a different way of practicing karate.
Mikio Yahara

Karate has many fighting techniques as eye attacks, elbow and knee strikes in close-range, kicks to the legs and knee, et cetera. These are highly efficient and powerful.
Yashunari Ishimi

Kumite

All challengers were defeated by my father and Ohtsuka Sensei, as they were Funakoshi's senior students. After a challenge had been met, Funakoshi Sensei would explain karate-jutsu and highlight the mental and spiritual benefits of the style.
Yasuhiro Konishi

You can see that there are many differences between real combat and sport and this is visible in kamae, not only the physical guard but also the attitude.
Geshin Hironishi

It must be admitted that the proclivity to engage in combat is no less common in humans than in other animals. It is extremely doubtful that those enthusiasts have come to a full understandingly of karate-do.
Shigeru Egami

At a high level of skill, kumite becomes like a chess game, not a game of speed and power.
Avi Rokah

Sparring is something that instructors should know how to introduce to their students. It has to be progressive and be taught using the old swim or sink approach. Once you get hit a couple of times and don't

Karate Wisdom

get damaged, your confidence increases and you relax. That's when you get a lot out of your training. I love to spar hard. You liberate your body if you train hard!
Dominique Valera

Free-fighting or kumite develops what we call "external timing," a critical skill for combat—it is an integral part of the whole karate-do picture.
Eihachi Ota

When the time comes to fight, you must not think in terms of simply winning, but you should feel delighted that you have attained your long-cherished chance to compete.
Keinosuke Enoeda

The good karate practitioner puts themselves in a dangerous situation in their mind when they practice. This kind of mental rehearsal helps to increase the intensity of the workout. It also helps them to prepare for the real situation.
Hideharu Igaki

Resign yourself to the fact that you're going to get hurt. Accept it. But be confident in the fact that your opponent is going to get hurt a lot more than you.
Katsutaka Tanaka

Self-defense techniques are completely different that those used for kumite. If you approach a self-defense situation as you would a competition, you are going to be in big trouble.
Kiyoshi Yamazaki

Kumite

When I moved in close, the opponent couldn't hit me. If you analyze a punch, the fist is the fastest point and the shoulder is the slowest. If you stop the shoulder you don't have to worry too much about the fist. It loses most, if not all, of its power.
Yukiyoshi Marutani

Rather than relying on intricate applications of each technique in the kata—which may or may not prepare you for a fight—the concept of ikken-hissatsu teaches you to develop a punch and kick so strong that they cannot be blocked and a block so strong that it cannot be penetrated.
Randall Hassell

Hard style contact is not about beating people up, it's about perfecting basic techniques and learning control. The contact in kyokushinkai is graduated: light, semi, and heavy contact. You need to develop other qualities before sparring full contact.
Shigeru Oyama

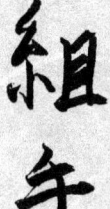

In karate-do, kumite is very important for the development of efficient, economic footwork, precise alignment, and fast, fluid action.
Tamas Weber

If a karate-ka loses a fight, we can't say that karate is not good but rather only that the practitioner has not achieved real karate skills.
Gogen Yamaguchi

To create changing circumstances we need a training partner; this is kumite. As far as I am concerned you cannot really say you can do a kata properly until you can make use of the techniques and principles of that kata against a determined uncooperative opponent.
Harry Cook

Karate Wisdom

I believe that karate is a form of self defense and that if we ignore close-quarter fighting, including grappling and ground work, we are poorer for it because many fights land on the ground.
Stan Schmidt

Traditional kumite is more relevant for the street because of the format. The true self-defense techniques can be delivered but controlled and not landed. When someone attacks you on the street, he is your enemy, not another competitor.
H. Ohtsuka II

Master Ohtsuka changed the traditional empty hand structure of kamae and placed the strongest hand forward—in a similar way of holding a katana. The angle of the punches was altered and sometimes we punch from a low stance in an upward angle. The principles of nagasu (side shifting), inasu (simultaneously attacking and defending) and noru (timing your counter to hit when the opponent's forward motion is at its greatest) are the foundation and building blocks of the wado style.
Hajimu Takashima

Free-fight or "all-around-karate" as I like to call it, is a good way to show your complete fighting ability in the ring and make some money on the side.
Jon Bluming

KUMITE

In the early days, there were competitions, but they were very different from now. If you were punched in the face, you did not show weakness. Instead, you would wait for an opportunity to hit your opponent back.
Kunio Miyake

If the dojo kumite is hard and of a high standard, it must be beneficial to your self-defense skills, but it must also be supplemented with thought and practice of simulated street type situations.
Malcolm Dorfman

Fighting has always been and always will be an important part of karate because that is where the true spirit of Budo is absorbed. Therefore, karate-do is an art because it allows us to reach higher levels of existence as human beings.
Masahiko Tanaka

I used sokuto-geri to the knee and leg a lot. It is a great technique to stop your opponent in his tracks, and I did get very good at it. I developed perfect timing and sensed when to throw it to stop the attack. This is a great technique for real fighting and self-defense because it causes a lot of damage.
Tatsuo Suzuki

Karate Wisdom

In combat, the highest level of skill is the ability to read and neutralize your opponent's actions before he moves. Similarly, the highest level of [skill in] self-defense is [the ability] to prevent a dangerous situation before it arises. This is true mastery.
Yashunari Ishimi

You should always think of your opponent as twice as strong as you, then you have to depend on timing and the efficient use of your body in every technique. You should strive to win by skill, not by power—that is what martial arts is all about.
Avi Rokah

When you stand face-to-face with your opponent, the first thing you want is to make him feel that your energy will overwhelm him. The second thing is not to miss any of his movement—even slight ones—and at the same time act as if you were engulfing the opponent's whole body with the inside of your hands and feet.
Keinosuke Enoeda

You need to experience the random nature of free-fighting, but the sparring should not always resemble that seen in tournaments. Sometimes competition free-fighting is over-refined from a self-defense point of view—that kind of sparring is a highly specialized skill used in a very artificial environment.
Harry Cook

At the initial stages of my kumite interaction at the JKA instructor's class, the fights were so real that my defense, speed and reflexes improved at an amazing rate ... simply due to necessity.
Malcolm Dorfman

Kumite

If you follow the Zen way, you will have the emptiness in your mind while doing kumite. Fear and thought disappear from your mind, and you don't feel the fear. In this moment, you are able to demonstrate your true power ... the power that is available only to you. No emotions, no thoughts about past and future. This is Zen.
Masahiko Tanaka

Simply sparring against one opponent is not enough; you need to face two or three opponents at once to get a realistic understanding of the chaos of fighting, and within the need for safety there should be minimum restrictions of allowable versus illegal attacks and techniques.
Harry Cook

It takes a real man who can take pain and is not afraid to do a hard workout everyday, punishing his body and going through a lot of physical pain and injuries. Full-contact karate is the first step to a complete fighter, but there are more aspects involved.
Jon Bluming

Karate Wisdom

When I started to train the whole idea of karate was as a self-preservation art, and not as a sport. The points were only awarded when the technique actually hit the opponent. The fighter were fighting and not playing a game. It was, by and large, much more bloody than any competition today. I also understand that at that time, competition was no more than a civilized version of street-fighting.
Alex Sternberg

Karate won't be an Olympic sport until the art is unified. The problem is that in karate we have many different styles and this creates a split and division among practitioners.
Dominique Valera

Karate competition has become increasingly popular, and gradually the true heart of karate has almost been forgotten. Modern karate-ka must think about the true root of the art and try to understand the essence of it deeply.
Keinosuke Enoeda

I also feel it is very important that an instructor know the difference between sport karate and self-defense—it will make a difference in how and what an instructor teaches.
Kiyoshi Yamazaki

The bottom line is that if you know how to use it properly, the art of karate-do is a school for the formation of human character. Competition is simply a game that emulates the element of surviving in life. It keeps it real and in proper perspective.
Yoshinao Nanbu

The truth is that in all oriental regimens for training and development, spiritual cultivation is the ultimate goal.
James Yabe

Sport

Evolution is inevitable, but the direction this evolution takes depends on the final goal of each practitioner. As long as you know where you are going, it's fine. Just don't get upset when you find you're a karate champion who can't defend themselves in a real fight.
Yuishi Negishi

In competition, the southpaw has an advantage over the right-hander because a left-hander will be constantly competing against right-handed opponents. This is probably why it is interesting to train kata in the opposite direction. It helps to balance the body and the practitioner's skills.
Seiji Mishimura

Technically, the changes have been very few and far between. I have seen changes in performance of various kata, and it seems to me that, for the most part, these changes have been implemented to make the kata more appealing to competition judges.
Randall Hassell

I am not totally against karate being practiced as a sport; but don't be mistaken, karate is not a sport. Certain technical aspects can be used and re-arranged for sportive competitions—that's all.
Shinpo Matayoshi

The European teams are much better in kumite than their Japanese counterparts. However, as far as understanding the principles and essence behind the art, probably not—besides a few rare and exceptionally knowledgeable and experienced Westerners.
Tamas Weber

The important thing is the way you chose and the success you have in refining and polishing yourself toward the achievement of your goal.
James Yabe

Karate Wisdom

One of the most difficult things to teach a student is the intent and commitment during a match. Once the competitor commits to a technique there is no turning back.
Val Mijailovic

All things evolve in life and these sports are no exceptions. You may like them or not, but you can't deny that they have a place in today's martial arts and combat sports. You don't have to agree with them but you can't deny them either.
Wally Slocki

Unfortunately, I see practitioners emphasizing only the sport aspect of karate. They focus only on trophies and prizes and not on the true spirit and essence of what the art is all about. They are becoming like baseball players.
Gogen Yamaguchi

Competition karate has to maintain the idea of ikken-hissatsu, which will keep the seriousness of true Budo and not simply allow the sportive scoring of points.
Masatoshi Nakayama

We have taken something which was never meant to be a sport, and have made a sport out of it. In this context I guess we could call it a

Sport

sport. No sport can be a Budo nor can a true Budo become a sport. So karate has split into two factions, Budo and sport.
Bill Dometrich

A coach is a motivator, a helper, an advisor—and not just a technical teacher. You must treat every member of your team equally, no favorites. Never lower your standards to treat someone special. Set an example to the players with your attitude and behavior because you have to find a common ground to bring everyone together.
Chuck Merriman

Japanese no longer dominate the sport. This is regulated competition, of course, but if you look at true Budo and non-sport karate, I think you will still find Japan still has the edge. Karate has evolved into a sport, like it or not. But there are still a rare few schools out there that disregard this part of training and teach the old way, which is technique, self-defense and personal development. The winners in this struggle are those that can do it all—the sport and the traditional training—even though it is a very difficult balance to strike.
Dan Ivan

Competition has a bad side. The worst thing is losing sight of your training just to win a trophy. Sometimes, the trophy gets to be the most important thing and that's not right. The student loses so much when they think like that.
Fumio Demura

Karate Wisdom

Much of modern karate is taught only as a sport, and it is noticeable that most of the larger karate associations choose their grading examiners from those who do well in competitions and award high grades to successful competitors, so the sporting values become more entrenched in the infrastructure of karate.
Harry Cook

Always train in the basics. This is something I noticed during all the past years; some top-competitors have very weak basics, they lack kihon. And after the competition years, it is very hard for them to progress in the true art of karate-do.
Teruo Hayashi

Although the training in karate-do is the most sporting and most complete, karate refuses to be a sport, but remains a martial art.
Henri Plee

Karate is a martial art that uses no weapons. This doesn't mean that I reject the sport aspect since I feel that's one part of the whole art.
Morio Higaonna

Unfortunately, karate today is neither a sport nor a martial art, and that's very confusing for the students. I think it would be better if sport karate evolved separately from the martial art side.
Hirokazu Kanazawa

I agree with the idea of karate becoming an Olympic sport. The sport aspect is a small part of the whole art—a small but important part nowadays.
Taiji Kase

Sport

Karate can be practiced for life but all these other combat sports cannot.
Kenei Mabuni

I attended what it was supposed to be a karate tournament, but saw no karate that I recognized. That day I realized how great of a misunderstanding the Americans had about real karate. I felt I had to stay and teach the art properly.
Takayuki Mikami

The sportive conception of the art is the responsible factor in losing many effective techniques found in the kata bunkai. They can't be used within the competition framework so practically nobody practices them anymore.
Minobu Miki

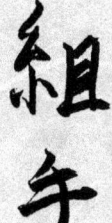

Karate matches are degenerating into mere exchanges of blows. Moreover, I cannot say whether the idea of free-fighting styles matches the soul of karate as taught by Master Funakoshi, the founder of karate-do. The soul of his karate requires quite a high standard of ethics. And we can't ever forget that.
Masatoshi Nakayama

I'm against a conception of karate as simply a sport. Competition is good but only while keeping the real values of traditional karate.
Hidetaka Nishiyama

Karate-do is Budo and Budo is not a sport. The real meaning of Budo is to go into life more deeply and improve physical and spiritual qualities through hard training.
Teruyuki Okazaki

Karate Wisdom

Sport karate has a part in the whole development of karate. Karate is popular around the world because of the sport competitions—but we shouldn't mistake the art with the sport because they are two very different things.
Tsuguo Sakumoto

I believe there are too many tournaments and that training in all aspects of kihon, kata and special drills should be adhered to. This means not just becoming a kata champion or kumite champion but becoming a champion of life!
Stan Schmidt

Competition techniques don't work in real life and in self-defense situations because the whole environment is different—but being a professional instructor means giving people what they want and need.
Takayuki Kubota

The value of training, irrespective of winning or losing, lies in how its benefits are personally applied to improving the quality of one's life. In my case, adversarial-type training and competition were my sanctuary and have been of immeasurable value.
Patrick McCarthy

Sport and tradition do have their place, but I use them in a different way. I balance them against all of the components in our practice.
Tino Ceberano

The art of karate is best taught and understood through

tradition, but it must shine through sport activities as well as self-defense.
Tatsuo Hirano

Competition karate is good. It has many regulations and is safe. It is a sport enjoyed by many people, especially kids. So long as it is fun then it is a good thing. But if poor etiquette and rude conduct emerge at tournaments then we should stop.
Akio Minakami

My personal feeling is many of us are selling our karate souls for Olympic recognition and Olympic affiliation.
Edmond Otis

We don't need to separate sport and the traditional element. Many young people like to have a chance to participate in sport karate competition, and it is very good for them. In the process, they make friends and grow up. But people cannot neglect the mental aspect of training.
Goshi Yamaguchi

Rules, referees, ring size, illegal techniques and the realization that losing the match will only entail going home without a medal pretty much invalidate sport competition as a testing ground for real self-defense skills.
H.Ohtsuka II

Karate Wisdom

I am not against sport karate if it is used properly. It is alright to participate and enjoy the element of sport and competition because it forces you to push yourself a little bit further, but it is wrong if you only focus on the sport and forget that karate-do is more than winning a tournament.
Hajimu Takashima

I noticed that Japanese kata champions are performing their kata differently in WKF championships than when they compete in Japan because the judges from the WKF have a different viewpoint on how the kata should be performed.
Kunio Miyake

Karate is changing, even in Japan the tournament karate is becoming more popular.
Koss Yokota

I believe karate is a Budo system with a sporting aspect for those Budo karate-ka who feel the competitive urge. However, this must then be the traditional shobu-ippon system to be defined as Budo with a sporting aspect.
Malcolm Dorfman

It is true that I have competed many times, but competition was always down on the list of my priorities when it came to the true values of karate.
Masahiko Tanaka

Sports karate is very popular now and many people consider karate a game. These people usually forget about karate immediately after competition. If necessary, I would like my students to be able to use

karate in real life, but I don't want them to treat it like it was strictly a game.
Mikio Yahara

If I continued to view karate only as a sport, as I did when I was young, I think that I would never have understood that lifetime exercise and character development actually lead to improvement in technique.
Shojiro Koyama

Sport is governed by rules for athletic reasons. Karate-do is fundamentally a study for the body, mind and spirit. Therefore, it requires physical and mental discipline.
Seinosuke Mitsuya

I am not against sport as long as the true spirit of the Budo stays during practice and training. Sport can be seen as a small part of the whole art called karate. That small part never is more important than the art.
Shigeru Sawabe

Karate is a martial art—not a sport. The sport aspect of karate has allowed the art to spread greatly. In itself, that is not particularly bad, but it sure brings consequences if you do not watch out.
Tetsuhiko Asai

Karate is not a sport, but some aspects of karate can be used as a sport activity in competition. Budo is the most important thing I teach.
Teruo Chinen

If competition today was like it was when I was young, then I'm sure that a lot of mental training should be done before getting into such type of confrontation. We weren't killing each other, but people used to get

Karate Wisdom

seriously hurt. Zen is a good way to learn how to deal with these situations.
Tatsuo Suzuki

If you are not interested in sport competition because of your age or orientation, don't enter a school that mainly focuses on entering tournaments. Ask questions when you visit the dojo. Don't be afraid. Once you know the kind of karate you want to do, then you have to find the right teacher.
Yashunari Ishimi

Competition has its place in karate, but its place is not in the regular basic training.
Yoshiharu Osaka

From competition to the real form everything changes.
Geshin Hironishi

Today, you see competitors that make it to the semifinals of a world championship because three or four of their opponents were disqualified along the way. That's not honorable—and honor is part of karate, part of Budo.
Alex Sternberg

Taekwondo people do taekwondo, judo people do judo, but karate people do shotokan, shito-ryu, kyokushin-kai, et cetera—and herein lies the problem. Without unification we'll never reach the Olympics.
Dominique Valera

Sport

Sport karate is a definite aspect of karate-do. Competition is not bad. It is good for the spirit. It is specifically good for the spirit when the proper etiquette—win or lose—is present.
Keinosuke Enoeda

The sportive aspects will bring more practitioners to karate, but it will be on the instructors' shoulders to teach the true essence of Budo in order to perpetuate the art in the proper way, for the generations to come.
Kiyoshi Yamazaki

Sport is a small part of karate. It can be used wisely to develop positive qualities in young practitioners—but if the teacher focuses too much on sport, students will be missing the whole picture.
Yuishi Negishi

Competition in karate is simply a sport. Nothing more, nothing less. But karate-do is Budo—and Budo is something that you can take with you for the rest of your life. Karate doesn't end when your competition years are over. It lasts until you die. If you approach karate like it was only a sport, you are missing the point.
Seiji Mishimura

Many students confuse tournament fighting with real fighting. Nothing could be worse than to have this false sense of security about one's fighting ability.
Shinpo Matayoshi

Karate is not, and will never be, simply a sport.
Tamas Weber

Karate Wisdom

There are many faces of karate, and sport is one of them. A bow and arrow can be used to kill or for an Olympic competition. It all depends on what the intent is.
Val Mijailovic

When you put your mind only in winning you are making a big mistake. Karate-do is mainly about learning to overcome defeat. When you lose is when you are facing your fears and your limitations. It is then when the true values and spiritual foundations of karate-do come to your life.
Gogen Yamaguchi

Karate is more well-known now. The popularity is because of sport karate, there's no doubt about it. I have no problem with sport karate because that is one aspect of karate training. But as we see in professional sports, we see a lot of athletes having bad attitude problems towards the referees, toward the other players, toward the judges. I just hate to think that this particular attitude would bleed over into karate sports. I think that karate sports should be based on courtesy, first and foremost.
Bill Dometrich

The tribalism, sometimes moronic behavior, cheating, drugs, and crass commercialism associated with much of modern sport has little appeal to intelligent adults. The sporting approach appeals mainly to young men and women, but eventually you grow up and need something a little deeper.
Harry Cook

There is nothing wrong with training these basic competition techniques and become a champion, but the art of karate is not a sport, it deals with self-defense and this is another subject altogether. You can't build a house with just two or three tools, you need a variety of tools to accomplish that goal.
Teruo Hayashi

Sport

Sport is good as long as it is regarded as a recreation that you can leave and then go back to karate Budo. Competition by itself is bad for the art, because you will understand nothing.
Hirokazu Kanazawa

Karate competition is very fashionable these days and it has allowed the art to spread. In itself, that's not particularly bad but it may bring some consequences if we don't keep an eye on it.
Taiji Kase

Competition is not bad, it's a modern aspect of the art. When you are young you want to test your skills, and competition is good for that.
Kenzo Mabuni

Even in Japan many karate-ka call their teacher "coach" not "sensei." They conceive it more as sport.
Takayuki Mikami

Freestyle fighting is good for the sport but there is the danger of digressing from other important aspects of the martial arts.
Minobu Miki

The art has to be used to develop the person and it's when the student trains only for competition when the direction is wrong. The secret is to train "in the art," not "in the sport."
Masatoshi Nakayama

I'm not against sport, but the problem with modern competition is that you don't need to feel Budo.
Hidetaka Nishiyama

Karate Wisdom

In modern tournaments I see important Budo aspects such as zanchin (continued vigilance-awareness), kokyu (breathing), tenshin (body shifting), and maai (distance), disappearing. If we don't control this, karate will end up being just a simple sport with nothing else attached.
Tsuguo Sakumoto

Sport karate is just one slice of the whole cake of karate-do, because what does one do after the sport side is finished.
Stan Schmidt

I take my students to as many competitions as possible to match them against different karate styles. I make them train harder discovering their weak points while they are under pressure and correct them. This is what I call "closing the gaps."
Takayuki Kubota

The competition mode totally destroys the ideals of the karate way.
Tino Ceberano

The "pros" are the sportsmanship and the international goodwill and exchange that result from sport karate. The "con" is the overspecialization of sports versus training in the whole art.
Tatsuo Hirano

Competition kumite has been the similar in every style for a long time as competitors adopt the movements of the champions.
Akio Minakami

Sport

The truth is, or at least my understanding, is that if karate gets to the Olympics, it will no longer be karate.
Edmond Otis

If karate becomes an Olympic sport, I'm concerned that something [traditional ideals] will be lost.
Goshi Yamaguchi

In a competition, the main objective is to deal with the opponent and win the match; in the street, the goal is not to be defeated and beaten.
H. Ohtsuka II

You must practice Budo karate and enjoy the competition without giving it too much relevance in your life.
Hajimu Takashima

I happened to choose traditional karate-do for myself because I wanted to practice the art my whole life. Combat sports are good when you are young and strong, but when you start to get older ... you simply can't perform them well.
Kunio Miyake

Karate will change and that is a natural process. It is our responsibility to keep karate at its best and improve it so we can hand down the arts to the next generation.
Koss Yokota

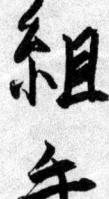

Karate Wisdom

If karate becomes an Olympic sport, karate will receive far more media exposure, but it will not be karate-do.
Malcolm Dorfman

Karate is not just a sport or a physical activity; it is a martial art and a way of life. A way of life is always part of us in every minute of our existence.
Masahiko Tanaka

It is undeniable that tournament technique is very different today than it was in earlier times. It used to be that karate opponents faced one another with a "one-punch, one-kill" front-line mindset. Now, karate competition is much more like a game.
Shojiro Koyama

Basically a "competition style" has been created, and all of the fighters look the same. The participants lose their own identity because the sport approach has been taken to the extreme.
Tetsuhiko Asai

Sport makes a student focus on speed and not the power behind the techniques. Everything evolves around who is the one scoring faster and not necessarily the one who is more powerful.
Teruo Chinen

Today, karate in most schools is only a sport, and this is wrong. I must agree that there can be a sport side to it, but the instructor should balance this and teach the student the two sides of the coin.
Tatsuo Suzuki

To stay close to the true essence of traditional karate-do, the requirements to score a point should reflect the important points of any given karate

technique. Otherwise, competitors will score with anything. Unfortunately, this is what is happening these days.
Yashunari Ishimi

Kamae expresses itself in a way that denotes the mental state and attitude (level of Ki), and even though sports competition blows may hurt, their goal is not to kill the opponent.
Geshin Hironishi

Champions today are the legacy product of that particular era, but they are also a more refined product, bringing together the extremes of both decades. Maybe the top fighters of the '60s were tougher than the top champions of today, but I believe today's fighters would probably defeat the best that the '60s could offer.
Alex Sternberg

In order to score you should hit, and of course it is going to be contact. That is karate. It is not fencing. I don't mean you have to knock you opponent down, but there has to be a certain amount of contact.
Dominique Valera

Technique, because of the tournament training, can become weak. The practitioner's techniques can becomes shallow because certain moves work best in sport karate.
Keinosuke Enoeda

Sport karate can only be practiced for a short time, but the martial art of karate can be practiced for your whole life.
Yuishi Negishi

To me karate should have never be turned into a just sport because it can offer much more than any sport. For instance, it not only teaches

Karate Wisdom

you to develop your mind, but also your character, Certainly, sports can do this to a degree, but karate, by itself, can do more to develop a person.
Seiji Mishimura

One direction is a sport, and the other is trying to keep the old concept of martial art. These two different and distant concepts can't be evaluated with the same criteria.
Tamas Weber

It is important for the student to understand what they are training for. Tournament training is totally different than self-defense training.
Val Mijailovic

Through sport you simply can't understand Budo, because Budo is about life and death, it is about to kill or be killed. My goal is to teach students to understand karate-do in the spiritual way.
Gogen Yamaguchi

A desirable aspect of competition is that it is an area where a student can place themselves in a stressful situation with an unknown quality and quantity of opposition. Then they can evaluate themselves in light of the final outcome. An undesirable aspect is that competition is strictly subjective in judgement and is someone's opinion of your performance, not necessarily what actually took place.
Chuck Merriman

Sport

Sport training can be fun, but it is essentially unreal in that it has to work within a set of rules designed with aesthetics, safety, and audience appeal in mind. If the concept of self-defense is absent then you are not doing karate: you are simply performing some kind of military aerobics designed to instill obedience and group solidarity.
Harry Cook

To a certain extent, competition helps to improve your fighting ability—but in my time karate was full-contact karate; it was knockout karate. I like contact karate because it is a very good method of making you cautious and forces you to have your eyes open.
Teruo Hayashi

Sport is open and enjoyable. Karate is not always enjoyable, because it is never easy to do the right thing. Karate is for the self. In sport we win over an opponent—in karate, we win over the self.
Hirokazu Kanazawa

Competition might impoverish the art because practitioners tend to standardize the way they train, therefore creating a competition style. Fighters end up losing their personality and their training becomes competition-orientated.
Taiji Kase

The problem appears when you only train for competition or you perceive the art of karate only as a sport. To me this is a mistake and a diversion from the true origins and goals of traditional karate.
Kenzo Mabuni

Karate Wisdom

Today, even the most traditional Japanese arts engage in contests. Unfortunately, in order to win, many competitors do wrong things such as cheating, acting, et cetera. And, of course, this is completely opposed to the spirit of martial arts.
Takayuki Mikami

Karate-do is a part of Budo, and karate competition is a part of karate-do as a whole.
Minobu Miki

Don't ever let your emotions show in the ring, whether you are in pain because you made a mistake and got tagged, or are ecstatic about executing a superb technique. Never give yourself away.
Alex Sternberg

Sport karate is okay, but it is not the only aspect of the art. We must try to not lose the true essence behind everything used in the sportive aspects of karate. Karate is education. It is about spirit and not only about trophies and street fighting.
Tsuguo Sakumoto

Competition karate has moved away from the concept of one killing blow. Today there are other factors to consider in order to bring more people to the tournaments. And these might be damaging to the essence of the art.
Stan Schmidt

I don't think there's anything wrong with competition. What I really dislike is that it is very limiting as far as technique is concerned. And that is bad.
Takayuki Kubota

Sport

The future of karate-do is wide open for substantial growth and development. I see karate not only becoming part of the Olympic games but also becoming part of national education. We must create the future rather than let it happen and shorten the borders for international exchange and friendship.
Tatsuo Hirano

Competition-wise I think everywhere in the world is the same. Everybody is developing a high level of competition skill. But in Japan, the overall level is much more skilled.
Akio Minakami

The art is much more than training, competing, winning a medal and setting a record. Some practitioners who win medals are very good, but if they only think only about competition, they are not thinking about their attitude and manners.
Goshi Yamaguchi

Competition was exciting to me, and it was more of the driving force. Now, as an older person, Budo is more important as the driving force of my training. Karate and Budo are life experiences that never end.
Kunio Miyake

I personally oppose adding karate to the Olympics. I am sure the Olympics will make karate even more popular, and this can be a welcome effect to many instructors. However, I am afraid the downside outweighs the benefits.
Koss Yokota

I am against the type of competition that promotes the development of game karate.
Mikio Yahara

Karate Wisdom

To put it briefly, the aim of sports is to win, conquer and dominate the opponent. Losing is "bad" and therefore value is only to be found in victory. But, as Master Funakoshi's quote so eloquently explains, the value in the martial arts, such as karate, is to be found in the lessons learned from losing as well as winning.
Shojiro Koyama

Competition has changed a lot throughout the years. In the old days, it was more of a one-punch, one-kill [mentality]. We really were aware of any possibility and making a single mistake meant defeat. That is the true spirit of Budo, and this spirit can be maintained in modern competition.
Tetsuhiko Asai

Karate was never designed for sport. Yes, you can use the front kick and the reverse punch to score a point, and that may be enough for tournaments. However, self-defense is a different thing altogether. You can't build a house with just one tool; you need a number of tools.
Teruo Chinen

If karate gets into the Olympics, it will be extremely difficult to maintain the mental and spiritual side of the art. That's why I said that it would lose its content forever.
Tatsuo Suzuki

A scoring technique should have the basic technical elements required by the art; a tsuki is always a tsuki and a keri always a keri, but a competitor needs to deliver the scoring technique with balance, the right ma-ai (distance), kime, control, body

mechanics and the correct fighting spirit.
Yashunari Ishimi

In any normal sport the judge only assures himself that rules are followed and has no power to decide who wins, something that does not occur in sports karate where the judge can decide who has won.
Geshin Hironishi

The present champions have much more skill, they understand more about training, muscle control, psychology, and tactics and strategies, and their physical techniques are on a higher level than they were 20 or 30 years ago.
Alex Sternberg

Competition is a challenge, that's why it is interesting. It is a test of your own capabilities against a live opponent. You put yourself on the line.
Dominique Valera

In tournaments, all those techniques which you perform for points are not actual combat skills. True karate-do is not strictly for technique but for developing your mind—because a person learning technique without the mind is not good in combat.
Seiji Mishimura

Sport misuses the karate traditions when the competitors insist that they are practicing a martial art.
Tamas Weber

Karate Wisdom

I don't think the Olympics did much to preserve the purity and spirit of judo! In my opinion, it did exactly the opposite. In my logical mind, why would the outcome for karate be any different?
Chuck Merriman

I hope that Olympic recognition does not mean that karate will go the way of judo and turn totally into a competition sport where winning Olympic, or other medals becomes the be-all and end-all of the training.
Harry Cook

The competition system is improving but there is still a long way to go in order to achieve the right scoring system that encompasses both the Budo and the sport aspects.
Teruo Hayashi

Tournaments are OK, but the practitioner has to understand more than only sport. Usually the practitioner is disappointed when the point goes against him because winning is everything, and he understands nothing else. A person like this is very dangerous to society because he respects only himself.
Hirokazu Kanazawa

Sport karate is useful during your youth but the art of karate is for all your life. You shouldn't modify techniques just to score a point.
Taiji Kase

The sport competition teaches us a lot of thing that can't be learned in the dojo such as pressure in front of people, mental control in an strange environment, et cetera. But you have to keep the right perspective.
Takayuki Mikami

Sport

There are many inferior international judges who do not really know the kata's original methodology and content. Instead, they tend to look for and give higher scores to the kata that was performed using only strong physical movements.
Minobu Miki

I hope when I die and meet Sensei Funakoshi that he's not angry with me for introducing the sportive aspect into the art.
Masatoshi Nakayama

A long time ago they started to create rules for the judo until judo was not a martial art anymore. To prevent this from happening to karate we must have a widening of techniques, and not prohibit so many practical self-defense moves, like judo.
Takayuki Kubota

In the event of karate-do being admitted to the Olympics, I dare say that our competitions would be a drawing card for the spectators.
Tino Ceberano

In competition, you are only seeing who is faster and who scores the point.
Goshi Yamaguchi

Sport is good as long as the true essence of the art is not lost because of the sportive practice.
H.Ohtsuka II

The most important moments that remain in my memory are those times in which I realized that my opponent wasn't able to control the situation and his skill wasn't as perfect as mine.
Mikio Yahara

Karate Wisdom

I think that Master Nakayama might look at the ultimate destination toward which karate seems to be headed and perhaps conclude that the sports mentality has been taken to an extreme. In that regard, as the father of modern karate, he might be a bit taken aback at the direction taken by some of his "children," a direction he probably never envisioned when he pioneered modern Budo.
Shojiro Koyama

Today, competitors simply jump and throw techniques without real kime or meaning behind them.
Tetsuhiko Asai

The intense competition has meant that the instructors of the various arts have really had to polish up their skills. And they have "borrowed" techniques and ideas from other styles and systems to make what they are practicing and teaching better.
Teruo Chinen

Let's not forget that shiai kumite is an aspect of the whole kumite side in karate-do. It has regulations and many effective techniques have to be eliminated to prevent major injuries.
Yashunari Ishimi

SPORT

Olympic recognition for karate seems to be very important these days, but I'm concerned because I have seen judo lose control of the art when entered in the Olympics. It lost the principles of the founder, Jigoro Kano. Karate must keep its essence as a martial art and Budo.
Yoshiharu Osaka

Karate is a sport or a martial art—it is what you make of it.
Alex Sternberg

The competitive life of an athlete either in traditional karate or in full contact is very short. It is a simple passage of time. Karate is much more than simply a tournament or a kickboxing bout.
Dominique Valera

The true karate-ka should be searching for their true self. True karate has nothing to do with all that fanfare existing in tournaments.
Seiji Mishimura

The Western practitioner in a final match will jump and celebrate after scoring a point. In the true spirit of Budo, you must concentrate and stay calm and focused, keeping all your emotions under control.
Takayuki Mikami

If sports competition continues to diverge from the Budo aspects, then the realistic and original ideologies of karate-do techniques will be lost.
Minobu Miki

Karate Wisdom

The way we always competed was very Budo-oriented. Unfortunately, many associations that regulate the competition rules allow participants to do strange things. They must be trained to kill with one blow, but they also have to learn how to control their power and techniques.
Mikio Yahara

Think of yourself as a performer at all times because that's exactly what you are. Don't get nervous and rush through the kata; perform it. Let the kata bring out your personality. Believe in the form. You can't convince anyone that your performance is good unless you are convinced of it!
Alex Sternberg

The spiritual and artistic features of karate are frequently neglected in favor of a focus on competition and showmanship. Unfortunately, when we turn completely away from the original cultural ideals or our art, we risk losing its rich and beautiful legacy.
Shojiro Koyama

Competition karate is only a very small part of karate. I have great students who are tournament champions, but this doesn't prevent them from training real Budo karate.
Tetsuhiko Asai

I don't object to the full-contact karate or kickboxing scene, but for dojo training they should stick to one style and teacher. "Window shopping" is not good for martial arts. I believe that these kinds of events and activities have their place, but they are not Budo.
Teruo Chinen

Sport karate is good if we keep the essence of what the right attitude and real technique should be in a life-and-death situation. This is as close as we can get to Budo.
Yashunari Ishimi

Sport

I would recommend using a variety of techniques derived from the bread-and-butter basics. I emphasize this because it is your ability to consistently use the basics with imagination and skill that will enable you to win with a greater degree of regularity and with a minimum of injuries.
Alex Sternberg

Kata competition has many aspects of individual timing and personal movements. If the timing of kata changes, then the meaning of the movements changes.
Minobu Miki

When you retire from competition or pass the physical prime of youth, sports as a goal becomes potentially obsolete. And once one has mastered self-defense techniques, one may become bored with training and quit.
Shojiro Koyama

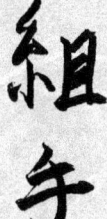

Without the competition influence, goju does not have high kicks ... only low kicks. So I think we've changed most for the sports angle.
Goshi Yamaguchi

In sport or competition karate, you can always find shortcuts to win. In traditional karate, there are no shortcuts of any kind.
Tetsuhiko Asai

Sport karate is not a series of spectacular techniques for a very simple reason; they leave you in incredibly vulnerable position. The idea is to show how precise and effectively you can hit, not how many fancy techniques you can throw at your opponent.
Alex Sternberg

Makiwara

まきわら

Karate Wisdom

I favor makiwara training. My dojo has several makiwara and next year we hope to install additional ones. It is the forge of traditional karate.
Bill Dometrich

Makiwara was invented because in early times, and in poor times in postwar Japan, they didn't have money or equipment. Makiwara or bag training is something you must do, otherwise you never know that your wrist might be weak and your hand might collapse when you punch.
Dan Ivan

If you want to learn to hit hard then you need to train on the makiwara or some substitute such as a punch bag or focus pads. It has been said that without "kime" or focus there is no karate, and without hitting something you cannot develop "kime."
Harry Cook

When we punch the makiwara, we are not only conditioning the knuckles but developing power, speed, and body coordination and punching mechanics. Everything comes together in makiwara training.
Morio Higaonna

I used to punch the makiwara more than 1,000 times daily, which is not correct. This kind of training is very important for karate but only with 50 or 60 full-powered blows per hand.
Hirokazu Kanazawa

Makiwara training the kind of karate that—unlike others—doesn't promote hands and feet as soft as a baby's because there isn't an emphasis on sport competition.
Teruo Chinen

MAKIWARA

The training with the makiwara post is to make the fist stronger by clinching the fist harder. This makes the technique more effective and the practitioner will learn the proper body dynamics of expansion and contraction of the body as it relates to correct techniques and stances.
Kenzo Mabuni

Makiwara is a very useful tool to develop focus. It also helps to forge a strong spirit, but pain is part of the process. If you don't know how to do it, it's easy to damage your hands irreparably.
Minobu Miki

He made us try the makiwara. I had trained before, and I had struck makiwara to toughen my hands. But many there had never seen the striking pole—then it was wound with tough rope.
Osamu Ozawa

Makiwara is very important, and this is very hard to understand because it doesn't offer squat for timing since it is a stationery object.
Ray Dalke

I use the makiwara. Practicing on the makiwara is very important for developing kime. The pain factor during training is something to consider. One must be careful, of course. But if you know how to train correctly, the makiwara will not only improve your overall technique but also teach you a lot about yourself.
Tsuguo Sakumoto

I teach two different styles of hitting the makiwara. First you must hit it relaxed and focus on the surface—I call this the "stopping style." The next method is to carry the strike through. You must make the entire body a weapon—even your toes!
Takayuki Kubota

Karate Wisdom

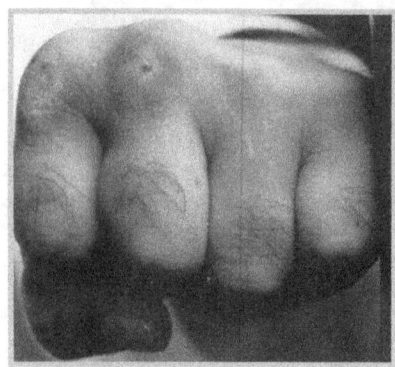

Makiwara training is indispensable to developing power, but it must be approached carefully with an understanding that we don't want to deform or disfigure our hands or damage them and then develop arthritis, which is often a by-product of such training.
Alex Sternberg

I don't see any point in using the makiwara. I'd rather hit a face than a wooden post.
Dominique Valera

Makiwara training is critical to developing ikken-hissatsu or one-punch stopping power.
Eihachi Ota

Every morning I would do 500 punches on the makiwara. It was not something I did to impress anyone. It was simply a single-minded attitude necessary to develop power and kime in my techniques.
Keinosuke Enoeda

Makiwara training is good for developing focus and power and strengthening the body, but it should be done correctly.
Keiji Tomiyama

Makiwara training is sometimes misunderstood. Some people simply think it is just to strengthen your fist and develop callused hands so other people are impressed when they look at your hands. Real makiwara training is much more than that.
Kiyoshi Yamazaki

Makiwara

Makiwara training was something that we did almost all the time. The idea is to condition your body so your limbs become real weapons when hitting the opponent.
Shinpo Matayoshi

Punching a makiwara 1,000 times with your knuckles bleeding is something that requires more than a simple ability to overcome pain. It is a mental ability, something that you have to develop throughout the years under the supervision of an authentic sensei.
Tom Muzila

Makiwara training and a fast and strong technique do not guarantee will efficiently deliver a lethal blow to your target. The way you train is the way you fight; and if the way you train is traditional, chances are the way you fight will be effective.
Tamas Weber

Makiwara has many benefits, but done incorrectly it can cause many health problems. I used to punch makiwara for many years and it got to the point that my hands were screeching when I made a fist.
Val Mijailovic

Many people think makiwara training is simply to develop big callous in the hands. That's wrong.
Wally Slocki

Karate Wisdom

I have done makiwara training for many years, but I have not reached [a level of] satisfaction from its benefits. With my knowledge of both the biological effects of using this and better ways to enhance my power, I have reverted back to corrective training and proper use of other implements in developing my personal skills.
Tino Ceberano

Makiwara training gives stances and strikes purpose. This training aid has the potential to strengthen and perfect stances and unite the whole body, mind and spirit.
Tatsuo Hirano

Target training is important to make sure our joints are correctly aligned, stable and coordinated with the breath at the moment of impact.
Akio Minakami

Makiwara training was optional, but most students did a lot of it. It was common for Okinawans to have a makiwara in their back yards. The makiwara were very abrasive. The hitting surface was made of rice straw ropes and it frequently would cut your knuckles.
Anthony Mirakian

The makiwara is an important aspect of training, and it should be used for achieving perfect form by practicing striking and relaxation techniques.
Kunio Miyake

The makiwara is a good training tool that teaches you how to make a tight fist and align your arm to your body and it toughens the knuckles.
Koss Yokota

Makiwara

Grandmaster Yagi felt that makiwara training was the best method to develop a devastating punch.
Anthony Mirakian

Makiwara training is good in moderation. However, overdoing it increases the chances of arthritis later in life and deforms the hands with no real tangible advantage over the conservative makiwara trainer.
Malcolm Dorfman

The makiwara is not only a tool to be used for conditioning, but when used correctly, it makes the body strong, especially the hips and hara areas. Makiwara training brings control to the technique.
Mikio Yahara

Traditionally, we had a series of supplementary training aids. They are classical implements that helped karate-ka to strengthen their bodies and prepare them for combat. The makiwara is one of them.
Ryusho Sakagami

You can practice on the makiwara and not develop callused hands. However, the tops of most makiwara in Okinawa were wrapped with 8 to 10 inches of rice straw rope and this would cut into the knuckles, leading to heavy calluses.
Anthony Mirakian

It is my opinion that many people tighten their arm muscles too long when training on a makiwara, as I see some practitioners push the makiwara after the impact. What I mean by too long is that the length of time is longer than what is necessary for a knockout punch.
Koss Yokota

Karate Wisdom

Makiwara training is very important. It is very helpful in working the legs and hips.
Shojiro Koyama

Makiwara training is not indispensable, but it can be useful if it is practiced properly.
Seinosuke Mitsuya

Makiwara training is not a joke because it can ruin your hands if it is not done properly.
Teruo Chinen

Makiwara training is necessary for real karate. If you want to develop strong techniques, you need to train with the makiwara.
Yoshiharu Osaka

It develops focus in a different way than other impact devices, such as shields, pads, bags, etc. Hitting the makiwara is a wonderful way to get a visceral appreciation for our traditions and the way that our art has developed and evolved, and it is different from the intellectual study of "the old days."
Edmond Otis

Training with a makiwara is very important in the development of proper impact and kime in the techniques, but it has to be properly taught.
Teruo Chinen

Makiwara

The well-constructed makiwara as an opponent is very, very difficult to beat. It helps hone a competitive edge while keeping the user quite humble.
Shojiro Koyama

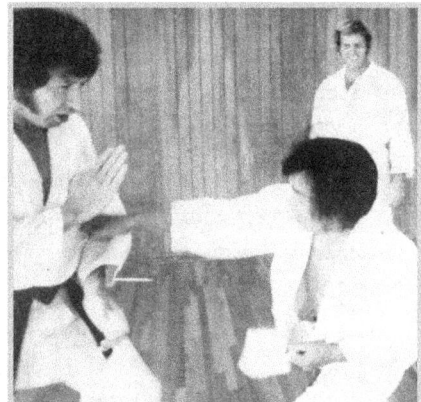

I believe that the makiwara should be used because it is another important tool that forges a strong spirit.
Kenzo Mabuni

Most people think that makiwara training only had meaning in the past because the hands and feet had to be deadly weapons, and with sport competitions taking over there is no need for that.
Minobu Miki

We used to do a lot of makiwara training back then in the old days. I don't punch the bag as much as I hit the makiwara.
Ray Dalke

After a year, the student can punch the makiwara over 1,000 times without a problem. Of course, sometimes we have injuries. People don't train like they should and make mistakes such as hitting the object improperly and breaking their bones. Unfortunately, it comes with the training. It happened to me many times.
Takayuki Kubota

Makiwara not only teaches the right kime but also the right distancing and the right impact feeling. The old training methods were created

Karate Wisdom

to improve karate technique and to make the human body a more efficient weapon—and not to win a beauty contest.
Alex Sternberg

You need to use the makiwara properly so your body develops that important aspect of all techniques in karate—kime. Without kime there is no technique in karate-do.
Kiyoshi Yamazaki

It is possible to have normal-looking hands and still develop a powerful karate punch. Many people misunderstand makiwara training. They mistakenly believe that the goal is to beat the hands and develop huge calluses, but the real emphasis is on strengthening the hands and wrists, so the wrist will not buckle if you have to hit someone.
Anthony Mirakian

The benefits you get from makiwara training are all important in a real fight, and you do not learn them in a non-contact kumite.
Koss Yokota

Traditional karate training places great emphasis upon the mind, and makiwara training helps this, because in many ways, it is the basis of the art.
Mikio Yahara

If the student is guided by a knowledgeable teacher, it is definitely positive. You don't want to hit the makiwara without having a previous understanding and knowledge of what your goals are.
Ryusho Sakagami

The makiwara is particularly good for older people because it trains the mind and the body at the same time, requiring sharp mental and

Makiwara

physical focus and speed training. Older people often fear becoming slower as they age, and the makiwara helps combat slowing and loss of concentration.
Shojiro Koyama

The makiwara is necessary to develop precision of technique and resistance at the moment of impact against an object.
Seinosuke Mitsuya

Training with a makiwara improves your timing, impact, and coupled with properly taught footwork, can greatly enhance your dexterity in striking on the move.
Teruo Chinen

The makiwara is not only good for your conditioning but it also teaches you a lot about the proper kime and the right positioning when delivering the technique.
Minobu Miki

We did not hit the makiwara an equal number of times with each hand. I was told that if you are right-handed, you should hit the makiwara three times as often with your left hand and vice-versa for left-handers
Anthony Mirakian

To me, training with a makiwara represents the last hope in maintaining the essence of the original spirit of traditional karate.
Teruo Chinen

Basically, makiwara teaches you the right technique. If you do makiwara training simply to develop big knuckles and calluses, you won't get any benefit from it because that's not the purpose.
Ryusho Sakagami.

Philosophy

哲学

Karate Wisdom

One of the basic tenants of Buddhism is that all things are impermanent; life is in a constant change from the day we are born until the day we die. I believe that a great majority of the traditional Okinawan and Japanese styles in America are being well taken care of by traditional American and Japanese sensei who live in this country.
Bill Dometrich

Martial arts always appealed to me because it was an individual effort and accomplishment. In school I was always too short for basketball, too skinny for football, and too slow for track. But martial arts just seemed to fit me naturally—it clicked for me.
Chuck Merriman

If you are sincere and you are teaching properly, they will come to you, and, like it or not, you are guiding and influencing their lives—a major responsibility that I took seriously. I actually changed from having personal selfish goals of doing karate—now I had to do it for my students.
Dan Ivan

Rank is something I really don't care about.
Fumio Demura

If you are interested in the ideals of Budo as well as practical self-defense, and by the way I don't see why they should be mutually exclusive, then the greatest enemy you face is your own over-inflated ego.
Harry Cook

When you truly understand your art after many years of practice and research, then you can look into something else and immediately have a greater appreciation of it because of your level of understanding.

PHILOSPHY

If you practice many styles without a base and without going deeply in one, you'll become a "jack of all trades, master of none."
Teruo Hayashi

It is evident that a great number of karate-ka and martial artists believe that they are seriously practicing martial arts and karate because they execute good kihon, well-done kata and, from time to time satisfactory kumite. But this is only a preparation; a sort of preliminary workout that is still a far cry from real karate.
Henri Plee

Karate teaching and training is not something easy. Everybody starts very passionately, with a lots of illusions, but due to the hard training only a few people continue.
Morio Higaonna

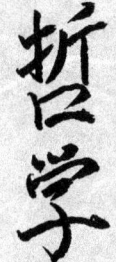

The karate that I teach is a product of more than thirty years of spiritual and physical research into the true meaning of martial arts. I always said that karate is a form of self-administered therapeutic massage. It is not just a sport.
Hirokazu Kanazawa

From the technical point of view, the art of karate has greatly evolved over the years but I think that part of the old spirit has been lost. And that is not good.
Taiji Kase

If you start training your mind from the very beginning, by the time you're old your mind will be strong and your body won't go down. If you're strong mentally and physically I believe you can face any problem in your life and come out victorious.
Kenei Mabuni

Karate Wisdom

A good instructor is not only a good technician. He must know how to teach a class, how to instill karate values, and how to deal with his student's psychology.
Takayuki Mikami

Karate offers a way of self-defense, firstly by technique and then by mental attitude. Through the practice of the art, an awareness of the self develops along with an understanding of how to avoid conflict.
Minobu Miki

Teaching these American students allowed me to realize that we needed more detailed explanations of "why" we were doing the techniques in the way we practiced them. The American students required explanations of the movements, so we started to analyze the movements and come up with theoretical explanations based on the laws of physics.
Masatoshi Nakayama

After all, that's what karate-do is all about—personal experience.
Hidetaka Nishiyama

There was no style. Master Funakoshi just called it karate-do because he wanted it to be called karate-do. But out of respect his students started calling it "shoto" which it was Master Funakoshi's pen name.
Teruyuki Okazaki

PHILOSPHY

Learners need only look within to discover the brutaly effective legacy handed down within these unique kata "time capsules." I am passionately dedicated to imparting this timeless message.
Patrick McCarthy

I don't think the karate has changed at all, it's still the same. The people have changed so the message has to be a little different now. If you want to win in both karate and life you must be very determined and very deliberate.
Ray Dalke

Karate is more than simply fighting, it's a whole art. Don't forget that the spirit of kata and kumite are the same. Kihon, kumite and kata are all of equal importance. You have to develop a strong foundation for the real karate to come out.
Tsuguo Sakumoto

Through the art of karate-do we learn to control the emotions and the physical training helps to achieve a calm state so we can be stable under pressure. In true karate, spirit is first and then comes technique.
Stan Schmidt

To find the true common denominator where all the Ways meet and apply it to Karate, this is what I search for. To find it is my ambition.
James Yabe

Karate Wisdom

I think they are attracted by the versatility of what I teach. I honestly don't know the main reason, though. The only thing I do is provide them with the best training and welcome them.
Takayuki Kubota

The Japanese are very rigid socially, and their karate reflects this attitude. The techniques they use must be just so.
Alex Sternberg

My wish is that karate will go in the direction of true martial arts principles, and competition does not necessarily contradict it.
Avi Rokah

For me karate was competition. It was a good and efficient way to compare myself with other competitors and find out what my level was.
Dominique Valera

An instructor must teach with a view to the students' abilities. But as one progresses and advances, additional training is critical.
Eihachi Ota

All practitioners should remember to train in true Budo karate-do. Do sport karate if you like, but always focus your mind and body on the perfection of yourself as a human being. This is true karate-do.
Keinosuke Enoeda

For most Japanese, karate is a martial art. They don't have the concept of a separate sport or of self-defense. But in America they tend to separate it into part sport, part self-defense, et cetera.
Hideharu Igaki

Philosphy

They say that studying martial arts is like walking on a stony road. It's very painful—nothing but pain. But that's how you learn the answers of life. The real truths come from fighting with yourself. No matter how good anything seems on the surface, you must be convinced—you have to convince yourself. That is the answer.
Katsutaka Tanaka

When Tani Sensei had taught his theory, he had always said that once mastered, these movements would become smaller and smaller and eventually invisible. Once these invisible, or internal, movements were mastered, there was no conflict between the modern teachings and the traditional teachings.
Keiji Tomiyama

Only when you give up the idea of rank will you realize that the study of karate is the study of your true self.
Kiyoshi Yamazaki

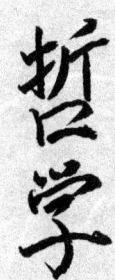

A true fighter cannot know the true gravity of martial arts until he has experienced it. I am probably the only postwar Japanese karate teacher leader to have undergone actual dangerous combat and, as a result, I have been criticized by so-called peaceful karate men.
Mas Oyama

I always want to learn something new. I want to research more into the relationship between basics—kata and kumite.
Yukiyoshi Marutani

I never considered myself better than any other human being so I did not have a problem being a Japanese karate instructor in Europe and competing against Europeans. I didn't want people to respect me simply

Karate Wisdom

because I was Japanese and supposedly knew more than Westerners about karate. I wanted to earn respect and so I put myself to test.
Yoshinao Nanbu

Karate should be taught as a complete martial art which allows individuals who feel so inclined, to compete, practice and train techniques that are suitable for sport competition.
Yuishi Negishi

Every new day is an opportunity to research new things and improve what you have been doing previously. Your expression of the art changes naturally as you grow older and hopefully wiser.
Seiji Mishimura

Physically, Westerners are just as good as the Japanese, but the Western student lacks the morality and ethics that a Japanese student has.
Richard Kim

Studying the history and development of Zen and how it has influenced Japanese martial arts will give the student a better understanding of how their art developed and why certain things are done in certain ways.
Randall Hassell

In America or Europe the teacher has to explain and elaborate when the students ask why they are doing this or that. Western students require an explanation for

Philosphy

everything, even if they don't understand it.
Shinpo Matayoshi

I don't want anybody's intellectual grasp of karate theory to exceed their physical ability to execute the art because this will make the head bigger than the muscles. Sweat first, think later—you must be physical to reach your mind, then you try to reach your balance.
Shigeru Oyama

Fear is not a bad thing if you understand it. My favorite definition of fear is: false, evidence, appearing, real.
Tom Muzila

Today my karate is like a tidal wave, with high-explosive power mixed harmoniously with the calm of the ocean sea. I strive to develop deeper and more focused types of movements based on internal strength and not muscle power.
Tamas Weber

Dreams are like plants: they only grow into reality when they are watered with sweat.
Joko Ninomiya

A front kick can be done 100 ways and each way will be right and within the form. Your way is the best way for you.
Val Mijailovic

Karate Wisdom

Sometimes a teacher is not simply the person who taught you how to punch and kick or a new kata. A teacher can be a situation—a certain moment where you have the clarity to understand what is happening and gain knowledge from that to be use in your life.
Wally Slocki

Too many people think the power of karate-do is only physical, but it is not. Karate relies on inner strength and power, an invisible power that is not recognizable by the human eye.
Gogen Yamaguchi

Karate-do is not only physical techniques but a philosophy of life. Age is not important for someone who really wants to train in karate. Karate is a life journey, not a destination. It's only when we look at it as a destination that we'll stop training.
Yoshiaki Ajari

Our study in the martial arts is in fact motivational. We must sustain endurance and develop tolerance and perseverance. Most importantly, we must make spiritual gains that come from the fighting spirit. This is zanshin or internal fortitude.
Tino Ceberano

I believe martial arts training is a medicine that can reach another dimension that is not obtainable by any other means.
Tatsuo Hirano

Our enemy is not some other place. Our enemy is in our own minds. We always have to project improvement for ourselves. This is what all these great people throughout history have taught. This is what the martial arts teach.
Tsutomu Ohshima

PHILOSPHY

If you want to learn the martial arts then you must learn how to control your temper and have good courtesy toward society.
Akio Minakami

Unfortunately, much of the essence and spirit of traditional karate has been lost. Since the advent of karate championships, many practitioners are competing to win at any cost.
Anthony Mirakian

The art of karate isn't simply about hitting things ... any more than playing a drum is just about using sticks to make a lot of noise. Karate is always about timing and distance. It is always about our relationship to our opponent.
Edmond Otis

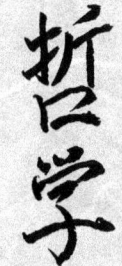

If an instructor focuses only on the technical and doesn't think about this side [philosophy] anymore, a student might have to think about moving to another instructor.
Goshi Yamaguchi

The teachings of the past are seeds for growth. Appreciate your sensei's teachings, treat them like seeds and cultivate them to be the truths of the future.
H.Ohtsuka II

Nobody is natural at karate because punching, blocking and kicking are not natural activities like walking. Now that I have said this, let me tell you that the technical movements practiced in the art of karate are based on scientific principles designed to get the most power, coordination, balance, et cetera from the human body.
Hajimu Takashima

Karate Wisdom

I loved to go around and show them the kyokushinkai style, and for those who didn't believe in the style and challenged me, I had to beat the piss out of them! What was funny is that most of them usually became dedicated students of our style.
Jon Bluming

I respect full-contact karate and kickboxing because those combat sports are extremely demanding and require a lot of dedication from the practitioners.
Kunio Miyake

Karate was little known in the 1960s and early 1970s. Judo and jiu-jitsu were more popular, so I initially taught both judo and karate. When the students saw the karate techniques—particularly the kicks— I got instant respect.
Koss Yokota

I feel a Budo dojo should emphasise tradition and self-defense over the sporting element but should not neglect sport training for those who are keen on competing.
Malcolm Dorfman

Karate is an art, and art is—more than anything—an expression.
Masahiko Tanaka

Budo karate, as far as I am concerned, is a situation in which I may finish my opponent definitively by one killing blow. My work basically

PHILOSPHY

consists in forming ways and methods to increase my technical level to the perfection I require and that is one blow should be enough to cause an opponent's defeat.
Mikio Yahara

The spirit underlying the arts practiced by the samurai was part Shinto and part Zen. This discipline was adapted from the Zen monastery and imposed on the martial arts elements and training. The most mundane act was to be performed with the utmost perfection.
Ryusho Sakagami

I have only trained in shotokan karate. However, after so many years of karate training, I have had the opportunity to meet masters of other styles and that helped me to better understand other styles and methods of karate.
Shojiro Koyama

To get the maximum benefits from the art, it is very important to learn how to put together and coordinate all the mental and physical elements of karate.
Seinosuke Mitsuya

The morale and mentality after the war dictated how all the practitioners felt and how dedicated they were to the training. It is difficult to explain, but there were mixed feeling inside each and every one of us.
Shigeru Sawabe

KARATE WISDOM

The important thing is to perform the technique with a certain spirit in a certain atmosphere. This is one of the main principles we were trying to develop at the old JKA.
Tetsuhiko Asai

The teacher should treat each student, taking into consideration the ability, age, and physical make-up and peculiarities of each individual. People are quite different—different body structures, philosophies, customs, and ways of expressing themselves—so it is natural that their karate will develop differently.
Teruo Chinen

I never worried about rank, so even if I was san-dan, I never cared about the next rank. Testing for 4th Dan was not on my mind at all. All the junior students began to push me to test because if I didn't test they would have never been promoted.
Tatsuo Suzuki

Looking back, I truly think all that hard training was extremely valuable for my future education, not only in the arts of Budo but for my life, as well.
Yashunari Ishimi

My father believed that if you walk a morally correct path in this life, then you are naturally following the divine way. If you train in karate in a natural way and master your body, you will expand your knowledge and experience, and establish a solid foundation for naturally living a morally correct life.
Yasuhiro Konishi

JKA karate tries to make the body stronger and the techniques more powerful. It is based on physics and principles of body mechanics.
Yoshiharu Osaka

Philosphy

It is important that karate can be practiced by the young and old, men and women alike. That is, since there is no need for a special training place, equipment, or an opponent, a flexibility in training is provided such that the physically and spiritually weak individual can develop his body and mind so gradually and naturally that he himself may not even realize his own great progress.
Gichin Funakoshi

If the quality of a person's life is changed for the better through the practice of karate, and they are able to share these benefits with their family and others, I am pleased.
Mitsusuke Harada

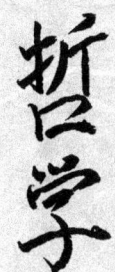

The sad truth is that many styles teach only the fighting art and neglect the spiritual aspects. And the practitioners themselves, who offer lip service to the spirit of the art, have as their real objective the winning of matches.
Shigeru Egami

Actually, analyzing competition in terms of real combat, it is better to receive the blow and afterwards strike with the idea of going through the physical barrier. Under those circumstances, do not be afraid, let yourself be hit and enter with decision.
Geshin Hironishi

The traditional martial arts are a type of "emergency training" for life. They teach us a method for self-understanding that helps us to control our weaknesses and accentuate our strengths so that we are able to be at our best when we really need to be our best.
Edmond Otis

Karate Wisdom

There are always those few select individuals who study a little of this and a little of that making green belt in one style and brown belt in another and soon proclaim that they are the master of their own style.
Bill Dometrich

Okinawa goju-ryu is an extremely deep style of karate which requires a great deal of time and effort. I don't think it is necessary to study another style of karate if the karate style you choose provides the proper self-defense structure within its framework of teaching. The old phrase "jack of all trades, master of none" immediately leaps to mind.
Chuck Merriman

It's hard to teach and train at the same time. If you train alongside your students, how can you correct them? And this is the responsibility of the sensei, to correct his students.
Dan Ivan

I think that people want too much too quickly. They want to run before knowing how to walk; or learn advanced techniques without mastering the basics.
Fumio Demura

You need to train in order to hold the ego in check, so in effect training never comes to an end. In terms of training with other systems.
Harry Cook

Philosphy

My perception of life, of the world has evolved, therefore, yes, I have changed and these changes definitely affect the art I'm teaching. On the other hand, I don't teach karate to please the student. I teach the art the way I think it should be taught. Period.
Teruo Hayashi

Style is preliminary conditioning to the particular ideas of the past or present master—a method of preparation or training and a mental and physical education.
Henri Plee

Karate is for all your life. The real purpose of karate is not to beat someone or to win against someone. Karate is a pacifist philosophy of self-discovery.
Morio Higaonna

Tai chi has allowed me to step outside of karate in much the same way as you need to step outside your house to fully appreciate it. From the inside, you do not have a complete view of it.
Hirokazu Kanazawa

At a certain level it is not the art but the person that's important. The styles converge, they share the same principles but it's up to the practitioner to make it work.
Taiji Kase

Karate Wisdom

Karate can't be understood quickly. Karate training doesn't stop when you remove your karate gi. Karate is for life.
Kenei Mabuni

The Japanese philosophy and the Western philosophy are different. Maybe the goal is the same but the approach definitely is not.
Takayuki Mikami

The ultimate goal of karate-do training is to make a better person, one who contributes to society as a whole. This is accomplished through disciplined physical and mental training.
Minobu Miki

Gichin Funakoshi wanted to grasp the essence of the different karate-do styles and incorporate them into his method.
Masatoshi Nakayama

It's very hard to please everybody. I support the traditional conception of karate-do.
Hidetaka Nishiyama

Karate-do or other physical discipline teaches them that if you don't sweat and work really hard for something, you'll never get anything. But if I used the same teaching methods that I did forty years ago, I wouldn't have any students!
Teruyuki Okazaki

Karate-do cannot exist without a body of moral philosophy to govern the behavior of those who embrace its empowering practice.
Patrick McCarthy

PHILOSPHY

I always knew that karate would only work if the body is in perfect condition, if everything in your technique is perfect. It would only work if everything came together as one whole unity.
Ray Dalke

If you only do kumite when you're young, you just develop physical techniques but not the art. You develop your body but not your brain. As a practitioner you have to strive to be skilled at both kata and kumite because as a teacher you must be able to understand and transmit the complete set of principles of these two elements of training.
Tsuguo Sakumoto

Karate is a never-ending journey of discovery. The minute I think I have mastered an idea or technique then new challenges appear. It is the climbing of the mountain that not only tests me, but gives me the on-going challenge to reach out and occasionally attain that enigmatic thing called excellence.
Stan Schmidt

It is true that some styles have weak points and where the student reaches the black belt level he might see those so he decides to go out and train in a different style. Some styles are very strong but they are weak in defense.
Takayuki Kubota

We study until we die, and we keep developing new insights.
Alex Sternberg

Karate is a journey—you have to keep looking and searching for things. Just make sure that whatever you are looking for makes you feel good inside. Because karate is, after all, simply the ability to uniquely express your inner thoughts with your exterior body.
Dominique Valera

Karate Wisdom

Karate is about discovering yourself and internalizing all the qualities required to become a good human being—character development, respect, discipline, ethics, and dedication.
Eihachi Ota

Winning can mean many things—good health, self-confidence, fitness, kindness, not only taking a trophy back home. We should aim for winning, but winning in life—as a human being—not only as martial artist and karate-ka.
Hideharu Igaki

I truly believe the old ways are the best and still work. Perfection in the martial arts is to make the mind and body work together. That's the final goal.
Katsutaka Tanaka

I do think that different schools are important because one cannot just learn one style of karate. There is no such thing as a standard karate. Different styles exist because of different historical ideas and principles. At the higher levels, all styles become quite close and similar.
Keiji Tomiyama

Today I focus on improving my spirit. When you reach a certain age, it is the spirit that keeps you going. Your body is left behind and your mind truly knows the limitations of your body.
Kiyoshi Yamazaki

The martial arts seek to unify and stimulate fruitful interaction between the physical and the mental, seeking perfection of man through fusing

the dualities of mind and body into a smooth, strong, finely-tuned instrument.
Mas Oyama

During my visits to Japan I had the opportunity to train with several other people who opened my eyes to different conceptual approaches to martial art techniques and philosophies. It was very rewarding experience for me, not only as a martial artist but as a human being as well.
Yoshinao Nanbu

The understanding about the functionality of the physical movement changes, therefore, the way of teaching it changes also. A karate-ka doesn't practice the art the same at age 25 years as he does at age 55. It's called "maturity."
Yuishi Negishi

It is only when you keep training and working hard that your true self comes out in what you are doing. It is this constant dedication to the tasks at hand that brings maturity and stability to your life.
Seiji Mishimura

Without a doubt, Hidetaka Nishiyama is probably the best karate master in the world. I have seen the man in action, teaching, explaining and demonstrating the art. He is simply great.
Richard Kim

Karate Wisdom

Karate has been the focus of my life since I was a child, so I don't really think in terms of "motivation." It simply is what I do—and I enjoy it.
Randall Hassell

The main objective of karate is to bring enlightenment, which includes humility and self-respect. It is not right to go out and look for trouble or to get into fights to get experience.
Gogen Yamaguchi

Self-defense used to be the essence of the arts, but that is in the past. I think that if a student wants just that and nothing else, then they can simply buy a gun or a knife. At least they will have much greater kill-power than a black belt.
Shinpo Matayoshi

You have to see you fear and get close to it. Simply don't let it go to your emotions. The main idea is that you must be in control, and this only happens when you face fear with your conscious mind.
Tom Muzila

Karate today has lost part of is fighting fluidity; the stances are more like movie choreography—very deep and stiff with a limited correlation to practical fighting.
Tamas Weber

Karate about growing and evolving. Evolution brings change and change is for the better. Karate is a living art, and therefore must change in order to exist.
Val Mijailovic

The traditional Japanese method is strict and hard, but if a student has the right mind and puts effort and time into his training, he will get

PHILOSPHY

good at it without a doubt. The Japanese approach is militaristic, but if you are capable of surviving it, the rewards are waiting for you.
Wally Slocki

Undertake the practice of karate-do as a lifetime journey so you can improve little things here and there without being overwhelmed by the idea of being an expert at everything. Don't fool yourself, you'll never be an expert at everything karate has to offer.
Gogen Yamaguchi

All your training must be based on deep honesty of what you are doing. Don't think you are superman because you know karate-do and you walk around quoting some Budo. philosophy—because one day you'll have a rude awakening. Don't lie to yourself.
Yoshiaki Ajari

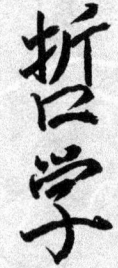

Do not stop at your expansion. Pursue the thoughts of your roots and origin and seek your truth but be mindful to reality.
Tino Ceberano

Although good hard training is the center of it all, building strong character and peaceful, respectful relations through karate is now the hallmark. In the past, the emphasis was on injury and killing for superiority.
Tatsuo Hirano

To me, it's important to try to face yourself directly, strictly and honestly. That philosophy has had a very strong impact on my life.
Tsutomu Ohshima

Karate should become better with time. If nothing changes then you must wonder about the teacher's practice. Isn't it the same with

Karate Wisdom

electronics or cars? Don't they get better every year? Open your mind and look at things around you.
Akio Minakami

Karate is not a purely physical art. It has physical, mental and spiritual aspects.
Anthony Mirakian

Karate is about striving to be at our best, our most focused, our most balanced, our most dynamic ... precisely at the moment our opponent is at his weakest.
Edmond Otis

Karate-do is more than just how well you can do for yourself personally. It is also how well you interact with the public.
Goshi Yamaguchi

Karate is a martial art, and as such is limited by the structure used by the art to deliver the physical techniques we learn. Self-defense is an important concept that cannot be limited at al by esoteric considerations. It is about self-preservation. That's what old traditional karate has always been about.
H. Ohtsuka II

PHILOSPHY

Many people think that basics imply that these techniques—after a few years of practice—are no longer useful. And that is wrong.
Hajimu Takashima

Recently, I read several times that Oyama killed many bulls in his time. The jackpot was during a meeting between England, France and Japan when some commentator told a packed stadium that Oyama had killed 28 bulls in his life. How ignorant and stupid can that be!
Jon Bluming

Before Tani Sensei passed away, he insisted that the name Tani-ha shito-ryu should be changed to Tani-ha karate-do. I think he changed his karate's name because he was open-minded and wanted to make the style deeper by incorporating other styles. Eventually, it was not pure shito-ryu as he learned from Grandmaster Mabuni.
Kunio Miyake

My belief is that a karate instructor, at least a certified one, must be able to perform better than any of his students who may be younger or physically bigger and stronger.
Koss Yokota

Karate practice is about life and developing skills that serve one not just in the karate sphere but also in all walks of life. These skills extend beyond the obvious benefits of health and self-defense and encompass abilities such as improved focus and concentration and the discipline to endure life's obstacles.
Malcolm Dorfman

Karate Wisdom

Karate is a martial art and a way of life, not only a physical activity that has a sportive side to it. Master Funakoshi said karate should be used as a tool to develop and perfect one's character ... both physically and mentally.
Masahiko Tanaka

When a strong person loses, he doesn't feel any satisfaction, and he will never find both spiritual and psychological victory. However, victory and spiritual satisfaction could come later, because your defeat stimulates new feats. You try to improve your skill, and as a result, you win. In this case, you will understand that the victory is the result of your last defeat.
Mikio Yahara

The true Budo spirit is not something that you can put on and take off at will. It is something you become. It is in everything you do and permeates through all your acts. It puts us in accord with the flow of the universe.
Ryusho Sakagami

To fit the Western psyche, I tend to use more explanations and come at these explanations from many different angles, which is not really the traditional Japanese teaching approach. Japanese students are not used to as much explanation; they are more accepting of basic drilling without verbal clarification.
Shojiro Koyama

A true practitioner of Budo must study and practice his entire life. The study of the martial arts is similar to the research of modern technology; you never stop learning and studying.
Seinosuke Mitsuya

We used fingers to the eyes ands throat, side of the hand to the neck, instep to the groin, kicks to the legs and every other technique that

Philosphy

allowed us to seriously hurt the opponent. That's how we learned karate. It was a method of self-defense and not a sport.
Shigeru Sawabe

The only limit in martial arts training is the limit of the human body.
Tetsuhiko Asai

As an art of Budo, all styles and systems of karate-do lead to the same goal. So, in the spiritual goal ... there are no differences.
Teruo Chinen

You don't have to kick or jump high to do good karate. The art has absolutely nothing to do with that. Everybody has physical limitations.
Tatsuo Suzuki

It is very sad to spend not only money but also time with the wrong individual. You can make more money [if you throw it away on the wrong instructor], but you can't get the years back. Time is priceless.
Yashunari Ishimi

In Japan, the traditional approach is: "Don't talk. Train." Work hard in the basic techniques and you'll find answers by yourself. You'll find your own karate.
Yasuhiro Konishi

JKA karate is a system that is based on the expansion of the body and using the natural power of it to perform the techniques.
Yoshiharu Osaka

When you look at life think in terms of karate. But remember that karate is not only karate—it is life.
Gichin Funakoshi

Karate Wisdom

Karate-jutsu or karate-do? The distinction between the two must be clearly grasped. Karate-jutsu must be regarded as nothing more than a technique for homicide, and that, most emphatically, is not the objective of karate-do. When practicing karate-do, what is important is to be one with your partner, move together, and make progress together.
Shigeru Egami

An instructor teaches many students of different abilities and skill levels and grades. He must continue to train in his many kata daily, many of which the majority of his students may not know. Because of this he needs to train in his basics but not neglect his more advanced techniques while doing so.
Bill Dometrich

An ideal student/teacher relationship should contain the same qualities as any other successful relationship—mutual respect, concern for each others welfare, consideration, patience, honesty, integrity, and openness.
Chuck Merriman

Karate changed in a major way after World War II, when myself and other GIs were stationed there. Early training was more combative, since Japan had just come out of about a fifty-year war. The attitude was a more severe war mentality, training was more serious and it took year for us to quit training and teaching as if we were going into life and death combat.
Dan Ivan

Philosphy

Martial arts training is not easy, but if you believe strongly enough in yourself, you can achieve anything.
Fumio Demura

Karate has in many ways lost the martial aspect, which I think is a mistake.
Harry Cook

Training should not stop once you remove your gi. Without the right spirit your karate will be of little use.
Teruo Hayashi

Narrow mindedness or a strict observance of orthodox static positions in karate can limit the practitioner to a mediocre level, which he will never surpass. A great master's quality can not be judged from a photographic perspective—it can't be understood in such narrow ways.
Henri Plee

Karate is spirit. Karate is life. Karate, for me, is like a cloud with nothing substantial to grab onto. You can do karate all your life and still find new meanings and new answers—that's why I practice every single day.
Morio Higaonna

Pure shotokan does not exist. The JKA practices a type of shotokan—but it is the shotokan of the JKA. Each master has a different view, a different brain, a different comprehension of things.
Hirokazu Kanazawa

Karate Wisdom

Karate is not about winning or losing but about character development. The character of the karate-ka is what is really important. Aim to develop the spirit and the higher self.
Kenei Mabuni

Karate is about effort and sacrifices. It is true that sometimes we make mistakes but we must always make a real effort.
Takayuki Mikami

Sport karate is limited in the type of techniques allowed, for the safety of the competitors. On the other hand, Budo is a way of killing an opponent.
Minobu Miki

To be a true master is to understand the soul of karate-do as a martial Way. Karate-do has grown popular these days, and its soul is apt to pass from our minds. We must strive to strike a balance.
Masatoshi Nakayama

Karate is art not science. It is an art that uses scientific principles. Science doesn't make karate. I learned my karate from the feel of the techniques.
Hidetaka Nishiyama

Karate-do was taught by Master Funakoshi and Master Nakayama as a way of life. He gave us, his proteges, the "Shoto Ni Ju Kun" or 20 Precepts To Live By. The idea of those is that karate-do is Budo and its goal is to develop character in human beings and to avoid conflicts.
Teruyuki Okazaki

The training methodologies for battlefield engagement, like street fighting, are completely different and require a totally different mindset

Philosphy

and training methods than what karate, as a defensive tradition, offers. However, if I were asked to offer any advice to someone looking to improve their safety on the streets I'd say, "Common sense and fast feet."
Patrick McCarthy

The bottom line is that you better be practicing the art and not just trying to learn how to fight. If you're trying to learn just to fight, you better look around because there are because some pretty tough guys out there.
Ray Dalke

In karate-do we have five maxims: character, sincerity, effort, etiquette, and self-control. All of them form our spirit and are different aspects of it. They are different kind of spirits and learning how to use the right one at the proper time is an art in itself.
Stan Schmidt

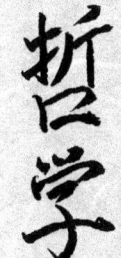

I teach gosoku ryu karate. I like to say that it may not look too classy but it is very effective. I teach how to use power when power is the answer, how to use speed when speed is the answer, and how to use evasion when evasion has to be used.
Takayuki Kubota

As an instructor you must set-up a training schedule or you stop training. Teaching is not training. Your personal development makes you into a better teacher.
Alex Sternberg

As a lifelong commitment, the practice of karate-do can change your life for good. To me the benefits of karate far outweigh the commitment of time and effort.
Eihachi Ota

Karate Wisdom

I believe the most important virtues specifically to martial artists are "mushin" or "no mind: and "muga" or "no ego." One has to empty ones mind to be able to understand the opponent's intention and get rid of ego to harmonize with the opponent in order to control him.
Keiji Tomiyama

You are always changing how to train, the techniques you select, and the way you see your art as your body and mind change with age.
Kiyoshi Yamazaki

Ignorance prevails anytime the facts are not present. The world was thought to be flat at one time. Taking a bath daily was considered unhealthy several years back. Centuries ago the earth was believed to be the center of the universe. Though all of these statements were held as truths in their own special time in history, man proved them wrong. As relevant facts made their appearance, the unknown became known. The mystical beliefs became non-mystical beliefs.
Mas Oyama

Sankukai was a very natural evolution of the shito-ryu method I was practicing already. That step in my life was not a way of saying, "I want to break free and do my own thing." It was a natural progression in my Budo journey and something I couldn't deny. If I did denied that evolution I would have been denying my own existence.
Yoshinao Nanbu

PHILOSPHY

Enjoy your training and keep practicing even if many things don't make sense in the beginning. Time brings understanding in the art of karate—you need time in order to mature and see things that are not visible in the first years of training.
Yuishi Negishi

Karate-do is similar to other martial arts in that it contains the knowledge, methods and skills—but the rest depends on the student's patience, endurance and personality in confronting and dealing with violence.
Seiji Mishimura

Black belt rank is about attitude, dedication and character. These three aspects are even more important than the physical skill. The technical skill is simply the basic element. I don't care how skillful a person may be—if they don't have the right attitude and character, I won't give him a sho-dan. Period.
Richard Kim

I see karate-do as an art of virtuous people and a tool that people can use to become better human beings—physically, mentally, and emotionally.
Randall Hassell

The martial arts are a miniature of life itself—a model to live by. They involve all of the elements of living. What you have learned in the arts, through practice and understanding, you can hopefully apply in day-to-day living.
Shinpo Matayoshi

Karate Wisdom

You must train intensely until your mind becomes much stronger than your body. Your mind must be tempered—do not give in to pain or discomfort.
Tom Muzila

The thinking and strategy dictate the technique to be used; which in turn requires a special way to initiate the application of power suited to the tactics. It is this means of applying strategy in combat that creates different styles.
Tamas Weber

Change is constant and on-going. The ability to adapt to our environment is the most important aspect of training. Our environment requires us to change and thus survive.
Val Mijailovic

When you are very young and you have the time, then you can play with things but after a certain point in your life, you know what you want and how to get it so you just don't waste your time in useless things.
Wally Slocki

Karate is a tool, as in other disciplines, that most practitioners see as a motivational activity with a purpose.
Tino Ceberano

Movement is life and life is movement and my criteria for being natural with karate movements are under constant scrutiny and construction. This process required me to find more ways to be natural with the movements of daily life and work, integrating them with Ki and karate in mind.
Tatsuo Hirano

Philosphy

Bruises heal, but mental scars don't. You have to give 100 percent because the idea of all this is to forge a new power in yourself, a new mental level. The ability to fight is really the lowest achievement of karate.
Tsutomu Ohshima

No style is better than the others, but the person practicing and the person teaching make a difference. Sadly I have seen many people with a limited outlook. We should always stay open-minded and be aware.
Akio Minakami

The philosophy of Okinawan karate—and goju-ryu in particular—is that in training the body the practitioner is also subconsciously training the mind. This is the tremendous richness that exists in true karate.
Anthony Mirakian

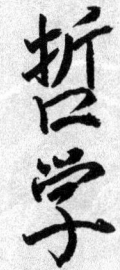

The true art of karate is a way of thinking, a way of life. In a way it can be describe it as an 'art of winning.' We 'win' when we get what we want in order to make this world better. But there are many ways of 'winning' and the higher level is not physical.
H. Ohtsuka II

Karate is not meant to be "perfect" on the outside. It's supposed to be perfect on the inside.
Hajimu Takashima

If you are a so-called karate teacher who must show what you preach, it is a must.
Jon Bluming

In the Western world, in some cases, karate is used as a way for parents to keep their children occupied or to teach them discipline. In Japan,

Karate Wisdom

from an early age, the discipline is already there and doesn't need to be taught.
Kunio Miyake

A student tends to follow an instructor's commands blindly without thinking about the technique he is performing. Improvements will not occur only with repetitions.
Koss Yokota

Nothing beats the quality of being hungry to succeed, be it in sport or in business or in any sphere, but it must be tempered with the correct attributes to complement and supplement this hunger. Karate is no different and necessitates a cool head and calm mind to channel this hunger into a systematic development.
Malcolm Dorfman

If karate training teaches us anything, it teaches us that the truth is always harder to take and less attractive than we would like.
Masahiko Tanaka

Some people think that the tradition of karate came from Buddhism and karate has a connection with the absolute, space and universe, but I don't believe in that. My philosophy is to knock my opponent out with one technique. One finishing blow!
Mikio Yahara

PHILOSPHY

It is important that a martial art instructor foster a sense of self-responsibility in his students. For the students, the best way to learn is to practice, persevere and think about the intent behind the technique.
Ryusho Sakagami

My karate philosophy reflects my belief that under adverse circumstances and conditions of struggle, a person's true character emerges. This is true in life and in the microcosm of life that karate represents.
Shojiro Koyama

For every age and everybody, there is a better way to practice karate. It is not necessary to use the same method or approach for every single student. Each practitioner must take care of the details. This is the essence of traditional Japanese karate-do.
Seinosuke Mitsuya

Karate was never meant to be practiced only by young people. So, in my opinion, the idea of formatting karate for strong and physically talented students was not a very good move.
Shigeru Sawabe

Nowadays, we don't need karate like we did after the war; it is a completely different approach. Karate needs to be useful for modern society.
Tetsuhiko Asai

Karate Wisdom

Things are not so obvious like they are in other karate styles in which you can see through the techniques clearly. In goju-ryu, everything is in some kind of disguise.
Teruo Chinen

Doing sanchin up and down a dojo floor won't be useful to defend yourself in a serious situation in the street in which your physical integrity is at stake. You have to take everything for what it really is and then you'll be at peace with yourself and happy doing whatever it is you are doing. And this applies to everything in life.
Yashunari Ishimi

Just as it is the clear mirror that reflects without distortion, or the quiet valley that echoes a sound, so must one who would study karate-do purges himself of selfish and evil thoughts, for only with a clear mind and conscience can he understand that which he receives.
Gichin Funakoshi

Loyalty, spirit, a never-say-die attitude, and intelligence are the most important attributes of a student. Unfortunately, is very easy for the students to get bored with the art, but in many cases they are bored with themselves.
Bill Dometrich

Karate is something a person is, and not so much what they do. You can't cut all the different aspects into pieces since they are all one thing. You learn from your teachers and your coaches, but in the very end it is all about you. You have to try to be the best you can be and take responsibility for your success or failure. Karate is a tool that we use to train our mind, spirit, and bodies.
Chuck Merriman

Philosphy

It is necessary to look at Buddhist, Taoist and Confucian works to understand the thought processes which underpin the physical practice of the martial arts. More specifically, looking at the various codes written by Matsumura, Itosu and Funakoshi will indicate the points that need work and study by the karate-ka.
Harry Cook

The philosophy and the training will help the practitioner to cope not only with difficult situations but also to show the proper respect to every human being. And that is tremendously important.
Teruo Hayashi

Karate is sometimes difficult to understand; you may train for a long time, day after day, and find nothing. All of a sudden, one day, you find out that you have truly improved not only in karate technique but also in karate spirit.
Kenei Mabuni

The mental aspect or attitude is paramount in this aspect of karate-do. However, the physical side is more important in the beginning. You must push the physical side first using your mental power, then both start to interrelate.
Minobu Miki

Karate is always on my mind every minute of every day—it's always there. I don't think there has been a day that I haven't done karate since the day I started.
Ray Dalke

I don't think it is necessary for a person to train in Japan. Today, there are many good instructors here in the United States and all over the

KARATE WISDOM

world. I do think that if you have the opportunity to visit Japan it is a good idea to experience a different culture.
Kiyoshi Yamazaki

Nanbudo is not a synthesis of different martial art styles and it is not an eclectic approach to Budo either. It is a complete art.
Yoshinao Nanbu

From the Westerner's perspective, the Japanese are an anachronism. We are conservative by nature. We want to protect the Japanese historical culture of martial arts. Traditionally we have no interest in changing them. We have no interest in polishing the arts to make them better.
Seiji Mishimura

There are many benefits of the martial arts and a primary one is to develop self-confidence and a strong mind. When this is achieved a student can utilize that development to help others do the same.
Tom Muzila

Philosphy

Karate is a martial art and a martial art includes many lethal techniques such as the finger-jabs to the eyes and attacks to the throat that are very valuable self-defense weapons. This makes it too dangerous to become only a sport.
Tamas Weber

My theory is to clear the mind and leave the ego at home. The "no-mind" attitude always worked for me. Allow your body to react on it's own to the situation—your body knows what to do.
Val Mijailovic

Learning not only involves the mechanical aspects of punching and kicking but very other important things like hard work, discipline, diligence, focus, curiosity, and having fun. Your attitude will determine where you go in life. This not only applies to martial arts but to life as well.
Wally Slocki

To my students, reaching a black belt is something priceless. It is not a trivial thing. It is not a badge only of physical accomplishment, but a sign that a person has achieved a certain mental level.
Tsutomu Ohshima

Budo is to empty one's self through the martial arts; to be fully present here and now with no extra thoughts in mind. Just deal with whatever you doing "now" and that's all.
Akio Minakami

Karate Wisdom

The technical aspects are mastered earlier in life while the spiritual aspects become more apparent and are of more importance as you become older. I truly believe that age is an important factor in this matter.
Kunio Miyake

When an instructor points out the important element, students reply by saying "Osu," but I wonder how many are really making a conscious effort to do that. Each student should not only listen but also apply that point to himself in each step and movement he takes.
Koss Yokota

I don't advocate change for change's sake, and this is what has happened recently in the world of martial arts. People with a limited amount of knowledge put together a little of this, a little of that, give it a new name and [suddenly] we have a new, complete martial art system that will liberate all the practitioners in the world from the useless, traditional methods.
Ryusho Sakagami

A famous professional sports coach once said, "Winning isn't everything; it's the only thing." I don't think this type of mindset is compatible with karate as a lifetime activity. Failure is an opportunity for growth.
Shojiro Koyama

I want to return to the roots and to the original essence and reason of karate ... a time in which there are no limitations. Karate is not only for young people.
Tetsuhiko Asai

Karate is a self-defense method. Not only does it teach you how to use your body to protect yourself from an aggressor, but it also gives you the moral and ethical code to avoid confrontations.
Yashunari Ishimi

PHILOSPHY

He who would study karate-do must always strive to be inwardly humble and outwardly gentle. However, once he has decided to stand up for the cause of justice, then he must have the courage expressed in the saying, "Even if it must be ten million foes, I go!" Thus, he is like the green bamboo stalk: hollow (kara) inside, straight, and with knots, that is, unselfish, gentle, and moderate.
Gichin Funakoshi

Always be loyal to your original instructor and never, ever quit.
Bill Dometrich

Karate is a challenge. It challenges you on the physical, intellectual, spiritual, and psychological level. I suppose I am basically an addict, but I find there is always some new area to explore—a new challenge to face.
Harry Cook

Karate-do must be part of a person's life, not separate from it. The path of karate-do is not an easy one, it is full of struggle and disappointments. As in life, not everything always goes right—in fact it seldom does—but if we have the strength to pass these obstacles then we'll reach a higher level, not only as a martial artist but also as a human being.
Kenei Mabuni

Traditional karate is not about technique like the people like to describe, it is about attitude. It's about life or death and not about doing hikite when you punch gyaku-tsuki.
Takayuki Mikami

The teacher has to learn how to communicate with students of different levels in order to assure they understand properly what is being

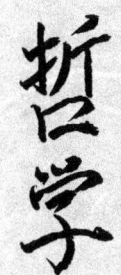

Karate Wisdom

transmitted. It is wise to have various approaches to teach the same movement or technique.
Minobu Miki

The soul of karate-do is the wish for harmony among people. Such harmony is based on courtesy, and it is said that the Japanese martial ways begin with courtesy and end with courtesy.
Masatoshi Nakayama

We [students] are brothers, not servants, and they [instructors] are not lords presiding over a medieval fiefdom.
Ray Dalke

It is not that I have changed the basic techniques but since I have studied different styles I understand their strong and weak points.
Takayuki Kubota

Karate is several things at the same time: a great physical activity, a martial art, a self-defense method and a great sport. We need to correctly educate future instructors because they will be the ones carrying on the art and the sport without losing the values of Budo.
Kiyoshi Yamazaki

In martial arts systems the difference between one whose mind wanders and the student who is attentive is much more apparent than in any other activity. A person must always confront fear head-on, otherwise it will overwhelm them.
Yoshinao Nanbu

PHILOSPHY

Every single karate-do instructor in the world influences and changes the art in some way according to his personality and point of view. That's a logical thing. There is nothing wrong with that. The art is nothing but the expression of the artist, and in this case the art of karate is a vehicle used by the karate-ka to express themselves.
Yuishi Negishi

Developing your body with pure self-defense in mind is not the main goal in modern training. We have gone a long way from bujutsu to Budo and some values have changed. It is part of a civilized evolution.
Seiji Mishimura

A martial artist must first set a good example for others to follow. Many times, we must sacrifice unselfishly for others.
Tom Muzila

There is no difference, in principle, between the martial artist and the soldier on the battlefield. The only difference is the goal for the actions and the tools used in combat.
Tamas Weber

The dojo keeps me motivated. It is a forgiving non-judgmental place. It unifies, and is a pool of energy that constantly replenishes me. It embraces all that is good and promotes learning and understanding of the physical, mental, and spiritual aspects of humanity.
Val Mijailovic

Karate Wisdom

Karate-do is the same as life, you need to keep learning to improve the way you deal with things. Life is all about change. If you don't keep an open mind, then you are setting yourself up for failure.
Wally Slocki

Education plays an important part on how an individual will be when grows up. Usually, when we get older, we become more selfish and greedy, with no time or energy for others. It is important to have a good educational system that doesn't spoil the young generation.
Tsutomu Ohshima

Japanese culture has many good traditions that can best be experienced in Japan. But it is not necessary to go to Japan to learn karate.
Akio Minakami

Karate is an individual activity.
Edmond Otis

Everybody must do it according to the way he sees the art, how it best applies to his dojo and what is best for his students.
Jon Bluming

For the sporting aspect, we focus on strength and physical abilities. For tradition, we focus our attention on knowledge and spirituality.
Kunio Miyake

There cannot be one ryu that transcends all styles, as our bodies and minds are all different. Can we say European fencing is better than Japanese kendo or Chinese sword fighting? Certainly not. Each karate ryu has the basic concepts of fighting style and methodology.
Koss Yokota

Philosphy

Karate was created and developed as a self-defense method. Funakoshi Sensei saw the flaws in trying to keep a warrior mentality in times of peace and developed a new approach to the art.
Masahiko Tanaka

There are no true losers among practitioners of the martial arts, because both victory and defeat are opportunities for spiritual growth.
Shojiro Koyama

The art of karate is practiced barehanded and its essence is to render an opponent unable to fight by using a single technique.
Tetsuhiko Asai

When you face death with the true attitude of Bushido, there is nothing to lose and everything to win. Karate-do helped me to maintain the warrior spirit and be ready for whatever came into my life … good or bad.
Yashunari Ishimi

Students of any art, including karate-do must never forget the cultivation of the mind and the body.
Gichin Funakoshi

Karate offers an opportunity to expand knowledge—not just the knowledge of Budo, but knowledge of different cultures and people.
Kiyoshi Yamazaki

The eclectic approach is very convenient for those who don't want to pay their dues. Definitely, this is not what I did when I created nanbudo. Everybody knows where I came from, what I did, what I accomplished as a young karate-ka, and the years I deeply studied the arts before expressing my own perception of the principles of Budo.
Yoshinao Nanbu

Karate Wisdom

I am not afraid of the flow of time and of making changes without losing my center. Blind traditionalism lacks vitality and life. Traditionalism, to remain valuable, must be dynamic and open.
Seiji Mishimura

A good karate teacher has an excellent balance in their personality and their mentality.
Tom Muzila

The basic concept of karate is to use all the mental and the physical abilities of the human body as a tool for self-defense.
Tamas Weber

I teach all that I know. Knowledge does not belong to me. We will grow through the challenge of our students. Personally, there is nothing more rewarding than to see my students grow and surpass me.
Val Mijailovic

In my opinion, the art of karate is not the same as self-defense. Teach the art and the sport separately, the tradition separately, and self-defense separately.
Wally Slocki

In the martial arts, we are racing toward [a situation in which we will see] who can be the strictest with himself. The martial arts contribute to human society in this way. We are racing toward who can be the strictest with himself and honest with himself.

PHILOSPHY

This was the original idea in the martial arts.
Tsutomu Ohshima

Be calm. Keep a cool head no matter what. We realize our potential with a calm mind. Be strong. Keep a good spirit to withstand anything and just keep on going.
Akio Minakami

My motivation has always been to make myself stronger, both mentally and physically. As a young person, I was shy and the martial arts helped to build my confidence. As the years passed, the philosophies helped to motivate me in many directions and to achieve my goals.
Kunio Miyake

Different masters had different ideas and skilled technique, but no one master was perfect. There is always something you can learn from another style.
Koss Yokota

Karate fosters in us the ability to appreciate the learning opportunities inherent in defeat and loss throughout a lifetime of experiences, both good and bad.
Shojiro Koyama

Harmony among mind, spirit and body. This has always been the key factor for me.
Seinosuke Mitsuya

Karate Wisdom

I recommend to use your imagination when training and think about karate. Look at the things and the live creatures around you. Study them and try to absorb the knowledge they have.
Tetsuhiko Asai

The martial arts and karate-do are a vehicle and a prescription for personal growth. They provide a useful tool to greater understanding and acceptance of many things in life.
Yashunari Ishimi

In karate, the idea is to beat others in competition or a fight. In karate-do, the goal is to overcome your own limitations and become one in spirit and body.
Yoshiharu Osaka

To win one hundred victories in one hundred battles is not the highest skill. To subdue the enemy with out fighting is the highest skill.
Gichin Funakoshi

Karate training to me is like life, you just do it, you don't think about it. I don't approach karate training with a calculating mind. I know it's difficult but we must strive to do karate without thinking about other additional things such as fame and money.
Bill Dometrich

The proper study of karate-do should be for the purpose of developing yourself to your highest potential—mentally, spiritually, and physically. It's essence is to learn how to live correctly and to be a positive and beneficial influence on those who rely on your guidance.
Chuck Merriman

Philosphy

Performing karate like a machine, without the proper relaxation, correct posture and breathing, will cause problems. That's the reason why I make my karate "self- chiropractic." Karate should improve health, not cause injuries.
Hirokazu Kanazawa

The instructor should teach the art through current applicable ethics and the logic of their society. He has to accept the role of father to his students. In doing so he has a big responsibility to teach them the foundation of karate as well as the etiquette and morals. You must practice what you believe and believe what you practice.
Kenzo Mabuni

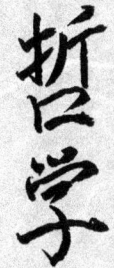

The karate practitioner must treat his body with utmost respect. It is very important for the modern teacher to study anatomy and physiology in order to understand how the body works. Then he can eventually develop teaching and training methods that help the student to improve their technical skills without getting injured.
Minobu Miki

Karate has taught me to look inward to face my own fears, better understand the pitfalls of ignorance and misunderstanding, and helped me overcome my own weaknesses in order to find out how to become the person I want to be.
Patrick McCarthy

My basic philosophy for my karate training is to keep good health and spirit in your life, and use it as motivation to train. When you can do this, your karate training becomes an integral part of a healthy life, on or off the dojo floor.
Kiyoshi Yamazaki

Karate Wisdom

Karate and Budo are not just aspects of my life but very major parts of it. Learning karate has to become a way of life. I have shaped my life toward learning karate and Budo.
Yoshinao Nanbu

A strong karate technique has nothing to do with the way your body looks. Physical appearance has nothing to do with real karate.
Yuishi Negishi

The person is always more important than the style they practice. What everybody must understand is that there are some styles that may fit better to some individuals than to others. You need to find what martial art fits you best.
Seiji Mishimura

Karate was a way of life—a life of training and devoted commitment with great respect for the sensei.
Tamas Weber

Karate is a part of my existence. It lives in all my worlds. I do not dwell over it, nor do I prioritize it. I enjoy it as I do my work and my family. It is a never-ending challenge like life itself. You can never know karate; it is like medicine—you can only practice it.
Val Mijailovic

PHILOSPHY

At face value, karate appears to be about fighting an opponent, but it is far from that. You should know goodness from bad because fists of justice are much stronger than fists of injustice. You should also get out of your own way by not fighting yourself.
Tatsuo Hirano

My black belts know that what they are learning is not for appearance or just for the use of competition or self-defense, but for their own spirit and soul ... for their lives.
Tsutomu Ohshima

Karate is a life long endeavor that can bring us happiness. If it doesn't, then we should look for something else to make us content. Either way, keep smiling.
Akio Minakami

Before you can increase your spiritual awareness, you must learn patience and realize that the karate experience takes many years of training.
Kunio Miyake

Teaching a class is a difficult task, so I do not understand why they wish to teach so soon. Maybe there is a perceptual glory in being a karate instructor, but I want them to realize that it comes with a big responsibility and obligation to the students.
Koss Yokota

Karate Wisdom

Perfection is something that sounds very good, but it is unattainable. By simply eliminating classical techniques and replacing them with boxing does not make a new method better or superior.
Ryusho Sakagami

I recognize that sports, entertainment and pleasure are very important, but philosophy and education is my field, my life's work. Personally, I believe that learning and studying are essential throughout life.
Shojiro Koyama

Life is very short, and I have a lot of things I want to do and accomplish. I'm a martial artist, not a politician. I always welcome anyone who wants to train with me, regardless of his association with other karate groups.
Tetsuhiko Asai

Karate helps you to understand how simple life should be: strive to happy. Life is very simple, but we [human beings] tend to make it very complicated.
Yashunari Ishimi

In karate as in life, you must be capable of working through adversity and overcoming your weaknesses.
Yoshiharu Osaka

There is no first strike in karate-do.
Gichin Funakoshi

To understand the spiritual aspects of karate through discussion is difficult. It is not something you can talk about and know.
Kiyoshi Yamazaki

Philosphy

There is no limitation in the understanding or technical development you can achieve in karate. The teacher should always try to improve their skill level by gaining new experiences, more knowledge, and a deeper understanding of what he is doing.
Tamas Weber

In Budo, or spiritual training through the martial arts, there is no graduation. There is no end to experience and wisdom. If you go deep into Budo then it is no different to the Chinese Tao and the Japanese Zen. It teaches us to do good and not evil, like religion.
Akio Minakami

I train for martial arts (Budo) and health purposes. I teach martial arts karate at my dojo but, if some of the students want to participate in tournaments, I do not object to it.
Koss Yokota

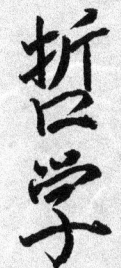

I can copy a Picasso's painting, but it doesn't make me an artist. To be an artist, and every karate-ka should be one, we need to learn how to express—in our own words—what we have learnt from our teacher. If the art is to survive, this is the only way.
Masahiko Tanaka

One principle, though, is important for everyone, regardless of their personal life stage or circumstances, and that is this: Study and planning are important and are your responsibility. Mindless existence is a waste of your valuable and unique life potential.
Shojiro Koyama

A good instructor keeps training himself all the time. He doesn't stop his personal training or his learning process, and he places emphasis on the basics movements and techniques.
Shigeru Sawabe

Karate Wisdom

I tried to develop a shotokan that would be practiced by people of all ages ... not only young and strong people.
Tetsuhiko Asai

Politics are bad news for all martial arts styles. Many great practitioners, with an enormous potential, leave the arts simply because they are tired of politics.
Seiji Mishimura

To try to research various elements of the martial arts prior to joining any martial arts school. With the various Web sites they may want to start there. I would also tell them to visit several schools, more than once if at all possible, prior to making their decision. Most importantly, I would tell them not to be impressed by flashy techniques, lots of trophies in the window, or be taken in by promises. Choosing a qualified instructor will be the most important thing they will do as a new martial artist.
Bill Dometrich

That's a hard one. My motivation and even my philosophy was to elevate my physical and mental stature. Martial arts does that while you're training without having to think about it.
Dan Ivan

Philosphy

I think that through hard work and an honest appreciation of your own strengths and weaknesses progress is always possible. Laziness and the ego, however, can prevent progress, so it is necessary to always try and keep what is known in Zen and Budo as "shoshin," the beginner's mind. This applies to both beginners and instructors.
Harry Cook

Karate-do training should constantly pursue higher technical perfection. Karate-do should be a lifelong endeavor which is enjoyable and beneficial, and not seen as a personal burden.
Teruo Hayashi

Karate training has to be done with heart and sincerity. It brings your body and mind together. That's the real karate.
Morio Higaonna

You must never forget that your the purpose of training is to master the art of karate, and to do so one has to develop perseverance and patience. This is the real spirit of karate.
Hirokazu Kanazawa

I don't think it is necessary for a karate practitioner to train in other arts such as judo or kobudo, but it definitely helps you to get a better appreciation of other arts, and how your style or system can be used if you face an opponent who practices those other methods.
Kenzo Mabuni

Karate Wisdom

Sometimes karate is boring and I understand. Everything is boring if you do it everyday for 30 years! The secret lies in not giving up, but in training the simple things until you feel better. That's the real test of Budo.
Takayuki Mikami

Today, we have a better knowledge of physiology and biomechanics and there is a better understanding of the legal and insurance aspects. Teachers are more inclined to look after their student's welfare and this is very good for everyone.
Minobu Miki

Karate-do emphasizes technique based on the practice of kata. We can continue to practice this martial art for a lifetime, no matter how much our physical strength declines. The more we practice, the more gracefully we can move.
Masatoshi Nakayama

I always say that you have to develop you own way, but this is where scientific explanations of each movement come in. If you copy Picasso or Van Gough or Monet, this might be OK just as a means for learning.
Hidetaka Nishiyama

I truly believe that those instructors who give into the demands for modernization are in reality cutting off their noses to spite their faces, and are destroying their greatest students by ignoring spiritual assets without which the martial arts become no more than murderous forms of personal combat.
Yoshinao Nanbu

PHILOSPHY

A teacher is recognized and accepted not as a martial arts expert, but as a man of dignity dedicated to the task of human betterment through the utilization of his talents. If a teacher displays these qualities, then he is a true sensei. If not, he is simply an instructor of fighting.
Seiji Mishimura

A good karate-do instructor teaches a student the way to teach himself; how to take all the elements of the art and weave them into his own experience and self-realization.
Tamas Weber

In the art of karate-do, kata is kumite and kumite is kata. You need both halves in order to be able to see the whole picture and completely master the art.
Wally Slocki

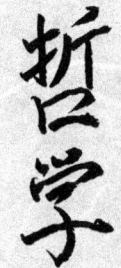

Grandmaster Yagi felt that free-fighting takes the true essence away from karate-do. In free-fighting, karate becomes a sport, and true karate-do is not a sport.
Anthony Mirakian

Karate-do is a life-long experience that has many levels of achievement. As you experience the mental and physical aspects at different stages in your life, you seem to grasp the higher levels of knowledge and use these tools in all life experiences.
Kunio Miyake

The unfortunate thing is that many of the tournament competitors believe there is not much difference between sport karate and Budo karate. I feel this is my job to teach my students how Budo training is different from tournament karate training.
Koss Yokota

Karate Wisdom

Funakoshi Sensei clearly explained that the goal of karate is perfection of character. Therefore, we have to look at it as a lifetime training and philosophy that involves the body, the mind and also the spirit.
Masahiko Tanaka

There is no perfect person, and there is no perfect style but the one that fits you and brings understanding and a peaceful spirit to your existence as a human being.
Ryusho Sakagami

I recommend Zen training. Zen training focuses on good, correct posture and breathing. Of course, it is a bit dangerous when an instructor tries to teach Zen to others without first having personal instruction from an experienced leader or teacher.
Shojiro Koyama

True karate is capable of adapting to the situation and changing accordingly. That is the essence of life. Change is simply the product of education. The more you learn, the more you realize other things.
Tetsuhiko Asai

Karate is based on hard training and sacrifice, but there is also joy and fun.
Yoshiharu Osaka

The development of your mind and heart turns out to be the main goal. This is not only important as a martial artist but as a human being as

PHILOSPHY

well, and karate is a good vehicle and a powerful way to help you to understand yourself better. Karate is a very special experience.
Kenzo Mabuni

The hardest thing to teach in martial arts is spirit, but it is the most important aspect the art of karate can offer to its practitioners. The mental and spiritual aspects of the martial arts can help one to overcome any kind of difficulties.
Takayuki Mikami

Attitude is the most important aspect. If the student is brought up the correct way they will understand that winning tournaments is not the most important thing, but that loyalty and having an open mind are far more desirable attributes.
Minobu Miki

The art of karate-do is about daily practice and if you follow this, the real truth will come to you because life is the same as karate training— a daily and constant practice.
Masatoshi Nakayama

All traditional karate is one— karate-do. Traditional karate is Budo. We must keep this philosophy.
Hidetaka Nishiyama

Training in Budo (of which karate is an integral part) strengthens the body, cultivates the mind and

Karate Wisdom

nurtures the spirit so that a Budo-ka can contribute to the welfare of humanity.
Patrick McCarthy

Now fighting is just out of the question although defending myself is definitely an option and I will do it with no hesitation—if the time comes it will be very deliberate.
Ray Dalke

The greatest masters always remain students. You must be able to forgive oneself and others, put the past to rest and move ahead. Every karate-ka has to think, "The way you conceive your future sculpts your present.'
Stan Schmidt

Even those who train in 20 different arts are not really respected by those who taught them in the first place. If I need to get surgery I want a doctor who is an expert in his field, not someone who has been jumping from one field to another.
Alex Sternberg

Karate training is a personal thing and a personal choice I have made. This choice and decision is not really a matter of public inspection.
Eihachi Ota

Karate is not only a way of simply punching and kicking, it is a way of life and as such affects all the facets of your existence. At least this is the way it should be.
Keiji Tomiyama

Important aspects of my karate teaching involve how and what is being taught. I feel it is important to teach children the importance of a good education.
Kiyoshi Yamazaki

Philosphy

When a teacher is teaching kumite and kata without teaching some of its philosophy and history, he is teaching in ignorance. I realize this is a harsh thing to say, but it must be said.
Mas Oyama

I don't know why people think that being a traditionalist is something wrong. Morality and ethics are something very important in order to have good citizen and a strong society. Creativity is not an excuse for blind rebelliousness. Disagreement for disagreement's sake is not being creative.
Yoshinao Nanbu

The body is trained through demanding karate sessions of kihon, kata and kumite, but the mind should be trained equally to counterbalance the physical side—this is only achieved through serious and dedicated Zen training.
Yuishi Negishi

It is important the young people learn how to control their lives—to stay calm and enjoy life without going wild. The right attitude and behavior will bring the right things to you.
Seiji Mishimura

I'm sorry, but I don't accept that. How can you give a black belt to a 12 year-old kid? He hasn't matured as an individual yet! It's impossible.
Richard Kim

I prefer to use the word, "spiritful," rather than "spiritual," because I don't believe there is anything inherently spiritual about karate-do.
Randall Hassell

Karate Wisdom

Ultimately, you want to be able to train to connect your mind, body and spirit with also your technical level. Where everything is working in accordance to one unit.
Tom Muzila

I truly believe that a lot of knowledge has been lost, not in a technical sense but in a more philosophical one. Losing these old masters is not about losing an unknown kata or secret application, but about losing the right training spirit, the correct attitude, and the proper state of mind to train karate-do.
Tamas Weber

The true spiritual aspect of karate-do is training. We do not have to sit and define it. By just doing, it becomes spiritual—overcoming fear is part of this growing process.
Val Mijailovic

There is a difference between kumite and trying to achieve good streetfighting skills. To me, karate as self-defense is a misnomer.
Wally Slocki

Life is a repetition of confidence and emotions. I believe that through karate training we can find the way to spiritual and physical exercise and exertion.
Yoshiaki Ajari

Philosphy

Maturity is the key and hence the practice must be a balanced circuit regime to suit the practitioner's schedule, physical condition and motivational incentive.
Tino Ceberano

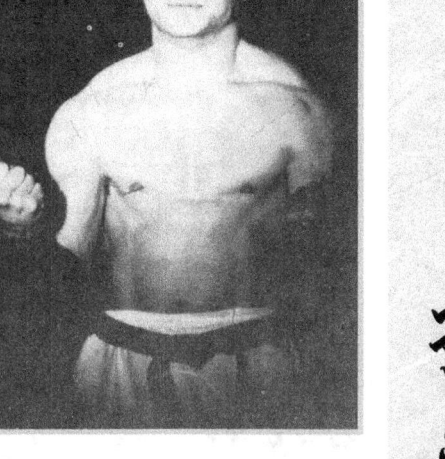

One hidden power of karate is its potential to develop you into a natural, uncomplicated being.
Tatsuo Hirano

When we die, we hope that we have had a wonderful life with few tears or sadness. We should appreciate everything we have until the last minute.
Tsutomu Ohshima

Karate is a personal experience in nature that needs nothing and no one else. It is always freely available, here and now!
Akio Minakami

Traditionally on Okinawa, goju-ryu karate is taught as karate-do or as a "way of life." "Do" is the Japanese pronunciation of the Chinese ideograph tao. Tao, or "the way," is the dominant idea of all Chinese philosophy, the foundation of the ancient Chinese world concept.
Anthony Mirakian

Karate is about how you can have a good life, but I'm not talking about money. I mean how you can be at peace with yourself.
Goshi Yamaguchi

Karate Wisdom

I believe the control of fear is one of the most neglected aspects of karate training. Teachers all over the world talk about technical control, but they don't talk about how to control fear and apprehension.
Hajimu Takashima

Students are the reflections of the teachers in many ways. You need to provide freedom, but at the same time, you must maintain a good structure for the art to grow. If the karate people had done that from the beginning, karate would now be the bigger than soccer.
Jon Bluming

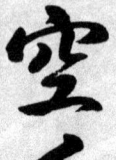

A karate-ka needs to remember to be humble, even after winning many championships. In my early days, the spiritual side of karate was strongly emphasized.
Kunio Miyake

It is said in Japan that it is better not to practice for two years while you search for an ideal instructor.
Koss Yokota

Focusing exclusively on tradition is difficult and must be balanced with a commitment to train in the basics and, for those who so desire, engage in competition and tournament karate.
Shojiro Koyama

The practice of karate-do begins at black belt level—not at white belt.
Seinosuke Mitsuya

Karate represents many different things. To me, it is a beautiful art that can be used as a physical activity to keep in shape and also a method of perfecting character.
Shigeru Sawabe

PHILOSPHY

In my approach to karate, I have been strongly influenced by the Chinese styles I have studied. The Chinese seem to be more natural and casual when doing things, and that affects the way they train and conceive the martial arts. In karate, we have the same movements and principles, but you have to look closely to discover them.
Tetsuhiko Asai

I have changed my teaching methods in some ways, but the essence of the training is the same. I may change with times, but the quality of what they receive is the same.
Teruo Chinen

Budo is a way to find life in the midst of death.
Yashunari Ishimi

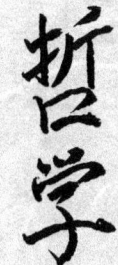

Don't try to do anything that your brain doesn't understand, but understanding things that your body can't perform may be detrimental for a true karate practitioner.
Yoshiharu Osaka

It is important to train karate for self-defense and not think that because you are a champion in karate competition that you can protect yourself.
Seiji Mishimura

We should keep the traditional styles or ryu independent and practiced separately. Personally, I am against the idea of mixing them up.
Koss Yokota

Practitioners of budo should seek out the fundamental concepts of Zen and apply them to their training.
Masahiro Okada

Karate Wisdom

In life, the goals that are worth keeping are the ones that take time and effort to achieve. Those things are not achieved quickly and require sincere dedication and good character.
Masahiko Tanaka

Everybody should ask himself the following question: "What is the most important thing for me in karate?" I think that we all should practice karate with the same spirit, mood and ideas.
Mikio Yahara

Present life satisfaction and mental stimulation are very important. Without intellectual stimulation, a human being becomes like an animal ... the spirit withers and the body soon dies. Training provides that source of stimulation.
Shojiro Koyama

The spirit that is facing death needs to posses a certain philosophy. He has to keep his mental and physical balance and not lose composure. In dealing with a life or death situation the technique is a very relative thing, not something absolute.
Kenzo Mabuni

Philosphy

I try to be the karate-do instructor that will teach students the correct, authentic traditional shito-ryu ideology and philosophy. I wish to have students who will inherit this virtue through my instructions.
Minobu Miki

The idea is to go deep into one art since after many years of training you'll be able to understand any other system and grasp the essence of it. Once again, I want to emphasize that this is the Budo attitude and approach.
Masatoshi Nakayama

For us the training was a war, and we didn't care who was in front of us—Japanese or Caucasian.
Ray Dalke

Your true opponent is your own mental limitation, not another person.
Shojiro Koyama

Karate Wisdom

We need strong characters for life as well for karate. Forging the body will develop the right Budo spirit.
Stan Schmidt

The practice of karate-do is the continual attempt at self-perfection, pushing the physical limits as far back as possible at every age.
Alex Sternberg

Karate-do, as any art in Budo, can only be realized through personal practice and not through words said by someone else.
Kiyoshi Yamazaki

To study karate to become great fighters is a lesser goal, but it doesn't mean we can't try to be good fighters. There is more to karate than just fighting. It's bad for a man to live with the thought of hurting others.
Mas Oyama

There is something I like to call your "sphere of influence." As human being, it is within this sphere of influence that you can be more efficient as an individual. You simply don't want to go beyond the boundaries of this sphere because all your true power and energy will be inefficient.
Yoshinao Nanbu

If you don't educate youth in the way of Budo, don't expect real martial arts to survive. If there is a lack of proper education, martial arts will suffer in the future.
Yuishi Negishi

Karate is for life. It is a way of life and a way of thinking. I use it and practice it everyday. It has to be used for when you find yourself in times of crisis. Karate teaches you to concentrate and think calmly under stress and strain.
Seiji Mishimura

PHILOSPHY

If you want a real shodan rank then go to the men who can teach you well, but accept from the very beginning that the road will be harder and more difficult than getting it from those who simply are interested in making money and not in the quality of what they teach.
Richard Kim

Teaching is a form of training, and after a person has been training for many years, the simple act of walking becomes training, too, because everything the human body does can be seen through the filter of karate training and thought of in terms of body mechanics, posture, awareness, and so on.
Randall Hassell

Once you take responsibility for something, you then have the power to change it. As Mr. Ohshima says, "You should eventually be able to look at yourself and your life and see no shame."
Tom Muzila

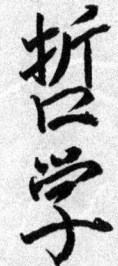

The discipline in the dojo, and the way you learn to respect the rules and your partner or opponent, will be reflected in the way you handle your private life outside the dojo.
Tamas Weber

Karate-do has come a long way and branched out to many forms—it has become a permanent entity in our society. It is associated with discipline and respect by the people of the world.
Val Mijailovic

Practice karate as an art and a sport but don't take it to the streets. It won't work. Street-fighting is a whole different ball game. The sooner you accept this fact, the better.
Wally Slocki

Karate Wisdom

As I have gotten older, mostly I just appreciate the benefits inherent in everyday practice, ordinary training and feeling good. That, in a nutshell, is the essence of lifetime exercise.
Shojiro Koyama

The philosophical basis for karate training is to become a good man who is one with the energetic realm of the Do, and I apply this way to all aspects of my life.
Tatsuo Hirano

Karate is a crystal of the human spirit and its heritage is a gem I intend to preserve. We are all trying to get out from underneath our stupidity, blindness, weakness and cowardice.
Tsutomu Ohshima

The true spirit and essence of karate-do lives on through those that were dedicated enough and chosen by the ancestors to preserve the heritage for future generations.
H. Ohtsuka II

I have come to understand and accept my weak side because I understand the importance of modesty and humility.
Shojiro Koyama

PHILOSPHY

Karate is a martial art and in every martial element you must experience fear and apprehension to some extent. It is important to have knowledge of it and know how to control it. It is the only way to understand what martial means.
Hajimu Takashima

I am 70 years old now, so what good does it do me if they write things and make me a so-called legend? And then you read on a website the most horrific lies about myself and other important Budo people.
Jon Bluming

Character is one of the most important qualities of a successful karate-ka. If a student has good character, he will build a good relationship with the sensei.
Kunio Miyake

The person who teaches you to discover yourself and your place in the world is not a coach. He is called teacher, master or sensei. He teaches you loyalty, courtesy, etiquette and all the important values that make a person a better human being.
Ryusho Sakagami

Karate is not just for strong people. It draws anyone who senses a weakness in themselves and wants to become stronger.
Joko Ninomiya

Karate Wisdom

Seek and strive to be the best. Do not let yourself get dragged [down] by anyone's words or by what only appears to be good.
Seinosuke Mitsuya

Any technique, regardless of how perfect it may be from a physical point of view, is irrelevant without the correct spirit. I'm not talking about anger or rage. I am talking about good spirit, which is something creative and positive. With it, we can surpass our physical and mental limitations and improve ourselves.
Shigeru Sawabe

I am now researching ways of training for life. I'm trying to develop techniques and training methods that we can use until we die. It's an unlimited world, and we must try to expand.
Tetsuhiko Asai

Karate should be for everybody from children to older people. Everybody can derive benefits from proper karate training, regardless of their age.
Teruo Chinen

Zen is difficult to teach in a few lessons. The student can't get an idea of what it is. It takes time and patience ... pretty much like good karate.
Tatsuo Suzuki

In combat, we need mindlessness and acceptance of what is; therefore, we learn to be in peace with the outside world. In dealing with this paradox of life-and-death, and peace in the midst of violence, we teach our minds to accept the duality of existence and focus on the now rather than trying to evaluate everything and try to find a reason behind it.
Yashunari Ishimi

Karate is a personal quest, and it is a personal journey.
Yasuhiro Konishi

PHILOSPHY

Budo is more than just learning how to fight.
Masahiro Okada

The secret is that you have got to just hang in there. There were a lot of tough times and a lot of kicks in the balls—and there are times when you've just got to stand-up for yourself.
Ray Dalke

The true karate exponent never stops training—this is my credo. I would like to see people going back to an old karate, where they are not so worried about egos and winning tournaments.
Stan Schmidt

Magazine exposure doesn't enhance my knowledge, nor does it bring more students to my dojo. Now, I would love to be on the cover of all the magazines, but it is not important enough for me to spend time and energy to pursue it.
Alex Sternberg

True feeling and right motivation are the foundations of Budo. There are things in tradition that are worthy to hold onto. They connect us with our past and make us better.
Kiyoshi Yamazaki

One of the experiences I remember most is when I came back from the war. All my friends in Paris were talking about a new master that had just arrived. They described him as fast, strong, impregnable, and very impressive. His name was Taiji Kase.
Tamas Weber

Zen mind is experienced only by those who are both hard working and lucky, and not every dedicated student will achieve it.
Masahiro Okada

Karate Wisdom

Style is not as important as the spirit of the art.
Ryusho Sakagami

Ninety percent of life is composed of the ordinary and the mundane. An appreciation for the mundane is what is missing in today's karate training.
Shojiro Koyama

In Budo, the gain is not visible— it is not that clear. The process is indirect and things should be discovered.
Kiyoshi Yamazaki

If I could, I would like to live the rest of my life as a hermit on some secluded mountain where I can train, eat and sleep when I want, without having any responsibilities or obligations.
Mas Oyama

Karate-do is Budo and as such it has to be internalized. Budo is for the rest of your life and it transcends trophies and medals. Budo is about life.
Yuishi Negishi

What is important in karate practice are the moral characteristics you get from it—endurance, perseverance, courage, self-esteem, self-confidence, self-control, and humility.
Seiji Mishimura

PHILOSPHY

A true martial arts sensei never stops learning until he dies and meets God. Until that very moment arrives, he is trying to help people in their journey to a higher existence as individuals.
Richard Kim

Cling to your roots, no matter what style you practice, and work together with your classmates and friends to create a good atmosphere in your dojo.
Randall Hassell

The meaning of karate-do and Budo is a way of practice with no real end or beginning—it is a perpetual stream of conceptions and principles.
Tamas Weber

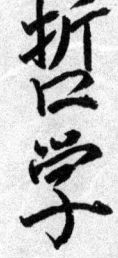

Sometimes people ask spiritual question about karate and I always answer with, "Go find a Buddhist monk and ask him." I don't get involved in discussing religion or politics. Karate, in my view, has always been an art and a sport.
Wally Slocki

If we are to follow the "Do" of karate, then it should be concerned with defense first—not attack.
Tino Ceberano

It makes me happy to think that maybe after 200 years somebody will still be practicing karate here where I have taught.
Tsutomu Ohshima

It is our responsibility as practitioners of lifetime educational karate to pass on the importance of the mundane aspects of life and training and to cultivate the patience that allows us to tap into the unconscious power of those mundane moments.
Shojiro Koyama

Karate Wisdom

We must realize or become enlightened to a better way and find out the secrets. This is not easy.
Akio Minakami

We all should remember that karate strives to protect the human life—not destroy it.
Hajimu Takashima

I love to teach and show dedicated students my ideas. If they listen and see the light, I am happy.
Jon Bluming

My karate training has always been for the evaluation of my fears, and my philosophy is to always conquer myself. Fear is an emotion that is always tested in all aspects of life, and my training—both physical and mental—is focused on the release of fear.
Kunio Miyake

It is also ultimately the instructor's responsibility to improve himself continuously so that he can provide the exciting training to the advanced students for many years.
Koss Yokota

I understand that there is an enormous gap between that philosophy of Budo and our modern way of life. But everything should be enjoyable and not evaluated in terms of money.
Tamas Weber

Karate training is a mirror of life, and the way you live your life must go hand in hand with the way your train. Your mind must grow as your muscles when you are young and strong.
Masahiko Tanaka

PHILOSPHY

Control your ego properly because the true enemy is inside yourself, and this is the toughest opponent to beat.
Mikio Yahara

Dedicate yourself to reach the higher levels of Budo and put your heart and soul into it. The key to understanding the art of karate-do and most other Budo arts is the underlying philosophy that runs so inseparably through all the forms of Japanese life.
Ryusho Sakagami

The technique and skill refinement imparted by my teachers must be in balance with the humility, enthusiasm and acceptance I am taught by my own lower ranking students.
Shojiro Koyama

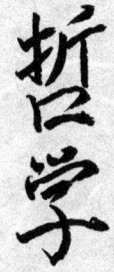

Kenwa Mabuni's goal was to try to gather as much knowledge as possible, and that's the reason why he studied so many styles and accumulated so many kata.
Shigeru Sawabe

It is important that the public has a clear idea of what is and is not the art of karate.
Tetsuhiko Asai

You have to cultivate the art and the true karate when you are young. You can't think that it will be there when you are older if you haven't taken care of it before.
Teruo Chinen

There is always something new to learn and experience but it's up to the student to seek and learn for themselves. The real value of acquiring an

Karate Wisdom

ability in anything, especially karate-do, is always trying to do better than you did yesterday.
Seiji Mishimura

Politics and organizations come and go, but karate training is for a lifetime, and that's where we should put our energies.
Randall Hassell

Karate-do is something that we own ourselves. It doesn't belong to any association or federation. It's ours. It becomes part of our own texture, learned in the bones, a kind of fixture of heart and body in cooperation with the mind.
Tamas Weber

Basically, I am teaching the same way I was taught at the Meibukan Honbu Dojo in Okinawa. I also keep the same attitude that permeated Grandmaster Yagi's dojo, and that means there is respect, cooperation, discipline and hard work.
Anthony Mirakian

Many benefits may be discovered along the journey toward self-improvement but it is only when one ceases to focus on external symbols of success and instead looks toward more meaningful goals of internal happiness that physical strength and spiritual fulfillment can be attained.
Shojiro Koyama

Karate teaches you how to gain and keep control of any situation in life. When you face a difficult task, push yourself into it until you can do it. Don't give up under pressure. Keep a good attitude and strong discipline.
Shigeru Sawabe

Philosphy

True karate cannot be discovered by simply talking and discussing philosophy and technique. Only through hard physical training and dedication can we feel what the true karate has to offer.
Yasuhiro Konishi

Just as the clear mirror that reflects without distortion, or the quiet valley that echoes a sound, so must one who would study Karate-do purge themselves of selfish and evil thoughts, for only with a clear mind and conscience can they understand that which they receive.
Gichin Funakoshi

I simply wanted to express karate in my own way. Karate has taught me to overcome my fears and myself and to get along with and work with others.
Tetsuhiko Asai

Karate—like a human being—needs time to grow. There is no end to expanding. Consider yourself always a student and never think that you are already there. Never give up.
Tetsuhiko Asai

Ohtsuka Sensei told us to continue training everyday and never stop. He practiced daily until his death. I try to imitate him and train everyday of my life. The only secret is to never stop training.
Tatsuo Suzuki

Karate Wisdom

I train in bo, sai and nunchaku. When you're using the nunchaku, your arms must be relaxed and soft—"empty" is the right word—no tense muscles. In nunchaku training if you move the weapon with tension, then you lose power.
Hirokazu Kanazawa

For the more advanced students I feel that kobudo offers great benefits. I feel that beginners should spend all of their time training in karate basics.
Bill Dometrich

Training with weapons is another dimension—another road to take for more dexterity and coordination. It is part of the total art and stimulating to practice.
Dan Ivan

I always say that kobudo and karate are like the two wheels of a bicycle. They work under the same principles.
Fumio Demura

It is important to train with weapons in order to understand the way the weapon is used. I think that some Westerners have gone further down this path than many Japanese, because of the nature of Western education which encourages the development of an inquiring mind.
Harry Cook

Nakaima Kenko taught me mostly the kama and the sai, and the empty-hand method of karate. In fact, I incorporated much of the ryuei-ryu theory into my own style. My other two kobudo teachers were Hohan Soken, from whom I studied the bo and kama, and Shiken Taira who gave me a lot of knowledge in several other kobudo weapons.
Teruo Hayashi

Kobudo

Kobudo helps the karate-ka to understand certain karate principles on a different level. But I recommend to start training in karate-do first, so you develop an strong base for the weaponry aspect.
Kenei Mabuni

Weaponry training is very good as a supplementary aspect. It must be extra, not the central part of your training.
Takayuki Mikami

Master Funakoshi never taught us kobudo but he introduced it to us, like history. For him karate was empty-hand, but I remember him saying, "If you ever have to use a weapon, use the best one to fight with!"
Teruyuki Okazaki

It is true that some of the methodology in the use of the weapons may be as obsolete, but the idea is to learn what was communicated from the old masters through kata and analyze the meaning and principles behind the weapon and its use.
Alex Sternberg

Kobudo builds the body in ways that empty-hand training can never do. It also demands a greater degree of mental concentration because the weapons are very dangerous to the student wielding the weapon—especially sharp weapons like the kama.
Eihachi Ota

It is not essential to train in weapons to progress in karate but kobudo training will help to develop the aspects which are equally essential for karate.
Keiji Tomiyama

Karate Wisdom

I think kobudo is an important part of training because it helps coordination and balance. The more you train, the better your spirit and confidence becomes, which helps your overall control. You introduce weapons gradually to the student to keep his interest, to lead him further into the true Budo. But then you become strict.
Kiyoshi Yamazaki

The old bushi arts involved weapons training, not only empty-hand techniques. They were different elements of warrior training and education.
Yuishi Negishi

Weapons training is very important because it brings into focus the frailty of life. Without weapons, karate loses the concept of art and degenerates into a sport.
Richard Kim

In kobudo you use your weapon differently against a bo or a sai. Your attacker's weapon determines the way you'll use your own weapon. It's simple common sense. This is where the real understanding of the art and one's own self comes in.
Shinpo Matayoshi

I studied weaponry but I don't think traditional weapons are practical for street defense these days I still teach them, though.
Shigeru Oyama

Unfortunately, kobudo practice has degenerated around the world. You can find people who just took a couple of classes and became self-proclaimed masters. Then they teach and give certification and ranking!
Teruo Hayashi

Also, if you practice weapons you don't need to lift weights or do most other types of supplemental training. Using weapons strengthens the body, legs, arms and grip, all of which are necessary in fighting.
Akio Minakami

By training with weapons we develop focus and concentration.
Val Mijailovic

Anything that a student can use, including a weapon, is good if it helps to increase strength, improve eye-hand coordination, or help with balance. All these factors are extremely important in empty-hand techniques.
Wally Slocki

Karate Wisdom

Kobudo training enhances many skills, including balance and evasion, directional power and specific hitting techniques. I recommend this totally.
Tino Ceberano

Weapons training will help the general conditioning of the body, but there is also a danger that may arise. This occurs if a student relies too much on the weapon for power instead of continuing his Ki training.
Tatsuo Hirano

Both weapons and empty hand should be practiced in order to fully appreciate Ryukyu bujutsu. Even the founder of shotokan karate, Funakoshi Gichin Sensei practiced weapons.
Akio Minakami

Training with weapons can give you an edge if you have to defend yourself against someone using a weapon. For this, it is helpful. For a sparring session or full-contact karate match, no way.
Jon Bluming

Karate and kobudo are separate and don't assist each other in the physical aspect. You can be a great karate-ka without training in kobudo, but it is very difficult to be an expert in kobudo without having previous knowledge of karate-do.
Kunio Miyake

Weapons are extensions of your arms. I have trained extensively with weapons, particularly the nunchaku. It certainly helped me with my karate.
Koss Yokota

Any supplementary training that helps coordination and skills must be of value. Understanding how weapons can be utilized will improve one's ability to defend against an attack with similar weapons.
Malcolm Dorfman

In some forms of martial arts, weapons are very important. I am training in an "empty-hand" style, and I consider myself in many ways still a beginner. If I ever finish my course of training, I will pick up weapons training.
Shojiro Koyama

Soke Hayashi practiced karate-do and kobudo with the spirit of the Japanese Budo [Yamato Damashii] for all of his life.
Seinosuke Mitsuya

It is my personal opinion that all practitioners who are san-dan and above should be using at least one weapon in their overall training schedule.
Koss Yokota

Karate Wisdom

Karate is the art of the empty hand. We don't include weaponry training at the JKA, but it is true that Funakoshi Sensei practiced several weapons like sai, tonfa, bo, et cetera.
Yoshiharu Osaka

I appreciate kobudo as a beautiful and effective category of martial art. But my feeling is that it is separate and different from karate, in the same way perhaps that judo and ju-jitsu are different.
Edmond Otis

Every weapon has its peculiarities, and the body has to adapt and become stronger when using the weapon. All this preparation helps a student improve the mechanics behind the physical movements of karate.
Seinosuke Mitsuya

A full study of kobudo is not for everyone but I strongly recommend some weapons training to everyone. My approach to kobudo is different from that of my instructors, though; in the beginning I use it more for supplemental training.
Fumio Demura

From a self-defense point of view I think you need to train against knives, chains, and bottles.
Harry Cook

Maybe it is not important for everyone, but it is for me. I truly consider karate and kobudo part of the same family. If I learn kobudo I will better understand the history of karate.
Hirokazu Kanazawa

KOBUDO

Training with traditional weapons helps students to develop important physical attributes that will improve their empty-hand techniques. In the process of learning how to use a weapon, the student uses the body in a very different way compared to the simpler empty-hand movements.
Yuishi Negishi

I see people thinking kobudo is outdated, such as karate's katas. The problem is not with the art, though, but with the observer's understanding.
Alex Sternberg

The kobudo weaponry is divided into three different categories; long weapons like the bo; short weapons like the kama, sai, and tonfa; and hiding weapons such as the nunchaku.
Fumio Demura

Once you drop the weapon and go back to empty-hand, you'll find that the body moves more in sync with the technique.
Yuishi Negishi

Photographs

Tsutomu Ohshima; 14.
Gichin Funakoshi; 16, 25.
Yuishi Negishi; 17.
Chojun Miyagi; 20.
Masatoshi Nakayama; 21, 276, 177.
Ryusho Sakagami's Dojo; 24.
Gogen Yamaguchi; 27, 68, 172.
Shinjo Masanobu; 29.
F. Demura & Don F. Draeger; 32.
Chuck Merriman; 33, 236, 301.
Richard Kim; 36, 80.
Kinjo Hiroshi; 89.
Y. Konishi & T. Ohshima; 37.
Henry Plee; 40, 72, 261.
Harry Cook; 41, 88.
Patrick McCarthy; 44, 84, 101.
Y. Ajari & H. Ohtsuka; 45.
H. Nishiyama, K. Mabuni, R. Kim & H. Shirai; 48.
Bong Soo Han, S. Ozawa, T. Hayashi, F. Demura. H. Kanazawa, T. Mikami & D. Ivan; 49.
Hidetaka Nishiyama; 52.
Y. Ishimi & Kenei Mabuni; 53.
R. Sakagami & S. Sawabe; 56.
Kenwa Mabuni & Gichin Funakoshi; 57
Stan Schmidt; 61, 154, 168.
Meitoku Yagi; 64, 284.
S. Mitsuya & T. Hayashi; 73.
Yoshiaki Ajari; 76, 143, 245.
Eihachi Ota; 77, 100, 135, 233, 241, 289, 300, 309.
Kenzo Mabuni; 81, 104, 240.
Kenzo Mabuni & Jose M. Fraguas; 129.
H. Ohtsuka; 85.
William Dometrich; 92.
Tom Muzila; 93, 167, 244.
Randall Hassell; 96, 113, 150.
Morio Higaonna; 97, 142, 180, 260.
M. Maeda; 108.
Malcolm Dorfman; 109.

Akio Minakami; 112, 158, 316.
Minobu Miki; 116.
Steven Casper; 120.
Tak Kubota; 121, 225, 257.
Koss Yokota; 124.
Y. Konishi & K. Yamazaki; 125.
James Yabe; 64, 128, 159, 232, 265, 277.
Hiroo Mouchizuki; 130.
Kenei Mabuni; 134.
Teruo Chinen; 138, 162, 273.
Masahiro Okada; 139, 281.
Anthony Mirakian; 146.
Teruo Hayashi; 147, 253.
Y. Osaka; 151, 256.
S. Mitsuya; 155.
Kenneth Funakoshi; 173.
Tatsuo Suzuki; 176.
Shojiro Koyama; 181, 268.
Shigeru Oyama; 183.
Mikio Yahara; 184, 224.
Fumio Demura; 188.
T. Asai; 197.
JKA Japan Kumite Team; 200.
USA Team 1980, Madrid, Spain; 201.
James Field; 205.
T. Tanaka; 209, 269.
K. Enoeda; 215.
Morio Higaonna (Hand); 220.
Yoshinao Nanbu; 221, 285, 293.
Y. Konishi; 237, 296.
Yashunari Ishimi; 248.
Goshi Yamaguchi; 245, 264.
Choju Hentona; 252, 317.
Alex Sternberg; 272.
Ryusho Sakagami; 288.
T. Sakumoto; 292.
Gichin Funakoshi's Group; 297.
Kunio Miyake; 304.
Shinpo Matayoshi; 309, 319.
Shimabuku; 314.
Seikichi Uehara; 315.

www.ingramcontent.com/pod-product-compliance
Lightning Source LLC
Chambersburg PA
CBHW071558080526
44588CB00010B/947